A Friend in Need
Is a Man's Best Dog

A Friend in Need

Is a Man's Best Dog

Selected Short Writings

Paul Fleisher

A Friend In Need Is a Man's Best Dog: Selected Short Writings

© Copyright 2017 by Paul Fleisher

Printed in the United States of America

ISBN 978-0-9991707-1-7

Cover design by Ryan Rich

Photo by Paul Fleisher

Thanks to Daniel Fleisher and Donald M. Zeigler for editorial assistance.

Published by Paul Fleisher www.paulfleisher.com

All rights reserved. The reproduction of any part of this book without permission is strictly prohibited. No form of this work may be reproduced, transmitted, or recorded without written permission from the publisher. Requests for permission should be addressed to Paul Fleisher, 2781 Beowulf Ct., Richmond VA 23231

Table of Contents

Humor

9	This I Believe
12	Lessons from Rats
15	The Teachings of Don Jones: A Yankee Way of Knowledge
27	Things Could Be Worse
32	*The Rock Garden Gone to Seed*
35	Seventeen More Reasons to End the Arms Race
39	Khomeini Ways Can You Say Ghotbzadeh?
43	A Dreadful Green Shade of Purple
51	Newly Discovered Work by Tolkien Published
53	So You Think You Have Tax Problems...
55	Two All-Beef Patties, Special Delivery
61	PBS Faces Reality

Education

65	The Fun Subs Have
71	The Reading Teacher at Work: A Revealing Glimpse for Parents
76	May I Have Your Attention, Please

80	Scoring Our Schools
85	The Educational Assembly Line: The SOLs are Limiting our Children's Education
90	The Myth of Our "Failing" Schools
94	Reading Your Rights: The Tangled Web of Special Education Bureaucracy
98	Teaching Evolution
104	Maggie Walker's Diversity Complex—written with Genevieve Siegel-Hawley
108	Un-American

Politics—The Arms Race and Other Campaigns

111	A Game Plan for Winning the Real Arms Race
116	Living In Glass Houses
120	It's Time to Stop Bombing Nevada
125	Binary Weapons: Reagan 1, Sanity 0
129	The Children Need to Know: Teaching About Nuclear War
135	Babes in Arms
140	Keep Your Fingers Crossed, Virginia
145	A Time to Remember, A Time to Act
149	Preserving the ABM Treaty
154	A Day in the Life

157	Pothole Economics
160	Restoring the Voting Rights of *All* Virginians
165	Why Not Raise Taxes on Those Who Can Afford It?
168	Armed and Unready
172	Why Loving Matters

Verse

| 175 | |

Leftovers

186	The Herring are Running, The Herring are Running
194	Book Reviews
202	Rush Hour
207	All that Glitters
212	A Modest Proposal
216	Solid Fuel
221	Pulling the Plug
225	In the Aftermath of Isabelle

A Friend in Need

(This page unintentionally left blank.)

Humor...or at least that's the intention

This I Believe

Following a tradition begun by pioneering broadcaster Edward R. Murrow, NPR aired a series of essays entitled "This I Believe," expressing the ideals that form the core of each contributor's personal values. In that exalted spirit, this I submitted:

I believe *believe* is spelled *believe*, and not *beleive*. It is *i* before *e* except after *c*, isn't it? The more I write them, the funnier they both look.

I believe light waves sometimes behave as particles, and that electrons and other tiny bits of matter sometimes act as waves. Or is it the other way around?

I believe for every drop of sleet that falls, a fowl crows.

I believe that if you took all the blood vessels from an adult human being and stretched them out end to end, that person would be very uncomfortable.

I believe Coke is better than Pepsi.

I believe that intelligent creatures from another galaxy visited our planet eight thousand years ago, and taught our Paleolithic ancestors to build electric waffle irons.

I believe those who repeat history are doomed to

misunderstand it.

I believe giving lengthy multiple choice tests to children every nine weeks will encourage them to become curious and help them to love learning for its own sake.

I believe listening to Mozart makes you smarter than eating fish.

I believe erections lasting more than four hours require immediate attention, medical or otherwise.

I believe opossums harbor deep and clever thoughts, but are unable to communicate them to us in a language we can understand.

I believe gasoline is much too cheap, and medicine far too expensive.

I believe there are more stars in the sky than there are grains of sand in all the world's oceans. Or is it the other way around?

I believe God so loved the world that He gave us both chocolate and coffee.

I believe there are weapons of vast and terrible destructive power hidden deep within bunkers and silos somewhere in North Dakota and Montana, in Texas and Arizona, in Virginia and South Carolina, in. . . well, you get the picture.

I believe in the power of love.

I believe that while the Inuit may have over twenty different words for *snow*, the English language has as at least twice as many for *frass*.

I believe the universe will get along quite nicely, thank you, no matter what I do or do not believe.

I believe I'll have another scoop of ice cream.

They said they liked it. . . but no sale.

Unfortunately, the market for humorous essays is extremely limited. There's the <u>New Yorker</u> and . . . well, there's the <u>New Yorker</u>—with one short "casual" per issue, a well established stable of writers, and a sometimes puzzling sense of what is and isn't amusing. Very few other publications use any humor pieces at all.

It took me quite a few years of returned manuscripts and rejection letters to finally face this fact. But even that hasn't stopped me completely. I'm just too much of a wise-ass at heart. At least I can still put a stack of these pieces together and publish them in this collection .

And so, here they are.

Lessons from Rats

Almost anyone who has participated in a leadership training workshop over the last few years has learned their "Lessons from Geese." Probably more than once.

Consultants believe these avian role models have a great deal to teach us about the importance of teamwork, sharing the effort, and encouraging one another through difficult times. A few years ago, it was almost impossible to check your email without someone passing on the geese's inspirational message. Just in case you are one of the few fortunate enough to be left out of the loop, just type "lessons from geese" into your favorite search engine.

However, these avian role models may not be as exemplary as our new-age trainers would like us to believe. These same geese have taken up permanent residence at our local park, hissing aggressively whenever someone walks too close and turning the path around the pond into a slimy green obstacle course. And of course, in recent years a few have had the misfortune to be sucked into the engines of jet aircraft. So perhaps it's time to look to other species that may have important lessons for us. Take rats, for instance…

Fact 1: Rats generate heat as their bodies metabolize nutrients. By huddling together in their nest, rats use only 50 percent of the energy they would need to stay warm individually. They also make lots more rats.

Lesson 1: Snuggle up close whenever you can.

Fact 2: When a rat gets shoved out of the nest, it suddenly feels the cold of being alone. It quickly squirms back into the crowded mass of rats, pushing aside any smaller rats that may be in its way.

Lesson 2: Force yourself into any position that offers an advantage. Shoulder aside anyone who may prevent you from achieving your goal.

Fact 3: When one rat is attacked by a larger animal, all the other rats scatter and disappear as quickly as they can. The one rat is sacrificed so the rest of the pack can survive.

Lesson 3: When trouble arises, save your own ass. Let someone else take the heat—even if you have to "nominate" him yourself.

Fact 4: As the rat pack searches for food and shelter, it allows nothing to impede its progress. Rats dig, scratch and chew their way through all obstacles, laying waste to their environment in order to get to a store of grain or a warm, cozy den.

Lesson 4: When there's something you want, let nothing stand in your way. It doesn't matter what or who else is destroyed in the process.

Fact 5: While foraging in a pack, rats claw and bite each other's hind legs and tails as they try to get ahead of those up front. This forces the entire group to maintain speed in its never-ending quest for food.

Lesson 5: To ensure everyone on your team is working as hard as they can, be certain each team member knows that there's someone else right behind them, nipping at their butt.

Fact 6: When the lead rat weakens, a younger, stronger rat challenges his authority, mauls him severely, and takes over his position of dominance.

Lesson 6: Claw your way to the top. When you get there, you'll get the best place to sleep, the best eats, and as much sex as you want.

Fact 7: When a rat becomes sick, tired, old or wounded, the other rats eat it.

Lesson 7: Never forget that no matter how successful you are, sooner or later you're going to be someone else's breakfast.

The Teachings of Don Jones:
A Yankee Way of Knowledge

I first met Don Jones on a wharf jutting out into the chill waters of Penobscot Bay. I had come to Maine to cleanse myself of the poisons of city life. With my expensive salt water tackle in hand, I had spent hours trying unsuccessfully to catch a fish.

One of the old fellows who had been taking the sun on the pier walked up beside me. He was a small man, with wrinkled, weatherbeaten skin, but I could sense a great reservoir of strength beneath his leathery hide.

He pulled a handline out of his jacket pocket. With a rapid series of movements he unwound it, baited the hook with some mysterious substance from another pocket, twirled the line above his head and let fly.

The hook and sinker flew in a great arc, landing in the water with scarcely a splash. As soon as the bait had settled, he began pulling the line back in hand over hand. Thirty seconds later, he pulled a huge flounder out of the water.

The old man repeated the procedure twice more, each time with the same results. Within five minutes he had caught enough fish to feed an entire family.

I must have been staring at him in disbelief, because he turned to me and said, "Now that's how to fish, Sonny

Buck."

"But how did you…? There has to be a trick. You're a wizard!"

"Ayeup," he answered, as he rewound the handline and replaced it in his pocket. He picked up the three fish, winked at me, and walked away with a sturdy, rolling gait.

I returned to the same pier every day that week. And each day the old man repeated his performance. The other men lounging on the pier seemed to treat him with great respect. I could see that he had some sort of special gift. For me he became the embodiment of a Yankee reality that was totally separate from the life I had known in the city.

It wasn't until the end of the week that I gathered the nerve to do anything more than nod a greeting to him. But finally I expressed my admiration for his abilities. He introduced himself as Don Jones. I asked if I could spend some time with him, and learn from him.

"What do ye think I've been puttin' on this show all week fer? Fer a city boy, ye sure catch on slow."

"You mean you'll take me as your student?" I asked, expecting to be turned down.

"Many are called, but few are chosen," he said cryptically. "One, two, three, you're it." He gave me a wicked slap on the shoulder that sent me flying into a stack of lobster traps. The other men on the pier nearly fell off their crates as they howled with laughter. I didn't see what was so funny.

"Let's go," Don Jones commanded. "Time's wastin'. You need to find yer third eye 'fore we can do anything' else."

Don Jones and a friend of his whom I came to know as Don Smith directed me as I drove about forty miles into the heart of Maine's farm belt. Don Jones finally told me to stop along the roadside beside a huge field of dark green, vine-like plants with small white and purple blossoms.

"Well, there it is," Don Jones said. "Go find it."

"But what am I looking for, and where?" I protested. I was already beginning to resent Don Jones's mysterious unexplained commands.

"Don't get all riled up, Sonny Buck. I said ye must find yer third eye. It's in that field somewheres. All you've got to do is find it."

I stepped into the field and began my search, although I had no idea what I was looking for. The strangely familiar plants caught at my trousers as I trudged through the field. I began searching row by row, hoping to find my "third eye" systematically. Don Jones and Don Smith had opened the cooler I kept in my car. They drank beer as they squatted by the edge of the road. They seemed to be getting a great deal of amusement as they watched me peer among the plants, which by now I had come to hate. After two hours of fruitless searching I had had enough, and I walked up to Don Jones and said so.

He just grinned. "Now who told you this learnin' you asked fer was gonna come easy? You must find yer third eye before we go any further. It's out there, I promise ye."

I went back to the search, growing more and more weary. The sun dropped low in the sky, and the air began to cool. I searched the entire length of the field's final row just as the sun set. Nothing. Overwhelmed with despair and exhaustion, I trudged back to the car. The two old men had finished off two six-packs; their merry mood was is sharp contrast to my own.

"Sonny Buck don't think his third eye is here," I heard Don Smith say as I approached the road. The men laughed. I was suddenly very angry.

"The boy's got no spunk," Don Jones agreed. A terrible dark cloud of rage swept over me. I rushed through the field, uprooting the hated plants. Then exhausted, I fell to the ground and clawed at the dirt with my bare hands. Tears of frustration streamed down my face. Suddenly my fingers struck something round and solid. I dug frantically.

Don Jones and his companion walked up and stood over me as I pulled my prize from the damp earth.

"See, I told ya it was here," he said matter-of-factly as I lifted up the huge potato.

Without warning, something snapped inside my brain, and I saw everything with amazing clarity. The plants that had looked so familiar were potato vines! I had found my third eye. Don Jones and Don Smith were rolling on the ground and laughing uproariously.

"Go on and eat it," Don Jones instructed. "Ye worked

hard enough for it."

I brushed the dirt from the potato and bit into it. Until that moment I hadn't realized how hungry I was. I sat between the rows breathing heavily, and quickly finished the potato. It was then that I had the first of many extraordinary experiences with a reality that is totally different from what we know in our daily urban lives. To this day, I still do not know how Don Jones managed to create these experiences in me.

I lay on my back and looked up at the night sky, which began spinning, slowly at first and then faster and faster until I felt I was being drawn upward into a swirling vortex. The wind howled in my ears, although moments before, the air had been completely still. Shadowy shapes seemed to fly around me, and flashes of light streaked across my field of vision. Great rumbling, booming sounds crashed around me, and I was drenched with moisture. As if from a great distance, I heard a voice calling "Far out! Faaar out!"

I couldn't recognize the meaning of the words, but the voice sounded vaguely familiar. Suddenly I realized that my own lips were moving. I saw myself lying in the middle of the field, as if a part of me were looking down from a great height. Everything started whirling again, and I was swept upward until I could see the twinkling lights of the coastline. Then everything grew dark. I was enveloped in a huge, dusky cloud, and the world disappeared.

I awoke on a straw mattress in a stall in what turned out to be Don Jones's barn. The light pouring in through the cracks in the siding seemed to sparkle and dance. I staggered out of the barn and into the adjacent house. Don Jones was sitting at the kitchen table, drinking a cup of coffee.

"Don Jones, Don Jones," I cried exultantly. "I flew last night, didn't I? I found my third eye and I flew!"

Don Jones looked at me with a cold intensity. "You think ye flew, because ye don't have yer full powers yet. All I saw was a foolish young man shouting and rolling around on the ground. Flyin' will come later. When yer ready. Now keep it down. I got a hangover that'd kill a moose."

Shortly after that experience I had to return to the city. But I visited Don Jones's Maine homestead whenever I could that summer, and the summer that followed. He taught me many things, although I often didn't appreciate their significance until months later.

Sometimes Don Jones would take me out in his diesel lobster boat to tend the traps. At other times, he would assign me various tasks around his farm. He told me it was essential to focus "perfect attention" on whatever I did, no matter how trivial or unpleasant it might seem. He explained that this was the only way a man could see through the "veil of the world" into the "veritable."

Don Jones gave me ample opportunities to practice this "perfect attention," as I spread manure on the cornfields, picked weeds from his garden one by one, or mowed the grass in front of his cottage with a pair of scissors. After each task was completed, he would inspect my work and point out where my attention had been imperfect, causing me to miss a blade of grass or neglect a chickweed seedling among the parsnips.

In the evening we'd sit on the front porch, and I would try to get Don Jones to tell me about the "veil" and the "veritable." He would just chuckle, shake his head, and tell me that when I was ready I would *know*. Beyond that he would say no more.

In mid-August of that second summer, Don Jones gave me the task of cleaning all the barnacles from the hull of his lobster boat with a nail file. Something in his manner told me this chore had a special significance. As I worked and sweated, I bent all my efforts to maintaining perfect attention. When Don Jones came to inspect my work, he examined the hull carefully and then said, "It's time."

I must have looked puzzled because, uncharacteristically, he explained what he meant. "Yer ready to fly. Tomorrow at sunset. Until then, ye must eat nothing."

As the hours wore on, I became more and more apprehensive about my upcoming flight. Also more and more hungry. Memories of a dozen other strange and terrifying experiences with Don Jones flooded my thoughts. I couldn't sleep.

The next morning, I drove to Freeport and bought a leather aviator's helmet, goggles and a parachute at L. L. Bean. Later that afternoon, when I appeared at Don Jones's door in my flying gear, he stared at me and then broke into another of his frequent laughing fits. "Put on your bathing trunks," he said.

I was mystified by his instructions, as usual, but I went

back to my stall in the barn and changed into my blue Speedo. I returned just as the sun was sinking behind the pines. Don Jones came onto the porch wearing denim trousers, a woolen work shirt, heavy boots, gloves and a veiled beekeeper's helmet. The slight chill in the air sent shivers of anxiety through my body.

Don Jones seemed to sense my discomfort, and gave me a disapproving glance. "Let's go," he said. He began walking down a path that led towards a stretch of marshland. I followed, my bare feet gouged by the sharp pebbles.

We walked in single file for about twenty minutes until we reached the edge of the marsh. Don Jones pointed to a log about fifteen feet out in the marsh itself. He told me that I was to sit on the log, and that if I could maintain perfect attention, I would fly. "Do not move, no matter what," he warned. I had seldom seen a more serious look on his face. He shoved me towards the log. I slogged across the sodden marsh and sat down.

For several moments nothing happened. By now most of the daylight had faded and all I could see were vague shadows. Don Jones was no longer visible, although I knew he was nearby.

I concentrated on perfecting my attention. Soon I became aware of a faint buzzing. It grew louder and louder until it seemed to fill my entire consciousness. My skin prickled with hundreds of tiny itches. The desire to scratch was overwhelming. I was about to give in to the urge when I noticed that I no longer felt the pressure of the log against my thighs and buttocks.

The buzzing grew louder. Cautiously I opened my eyes and found myself a dozen feet in the air, spinning slowly in a counter-clockwise direction and simultaneously moving towards a line of low trees several hundred feet away. I felt as if I had sprouted thousands of tiny wings. My skin was on fire with maddening itches, yet I dared not move to scratch.

Suddenly a huge, hideous flying insect appeared before me. I saw multiple images of myself reflected in its compound eyes. The creature hovered above me, its long proboscis pointing unwaveringly at my heart.

I began to descend. I landed gently in a grove of scrub pine. The air seemed to shatter into thousands of hovering black specks. Their high-pitched whine was deafening. I heard a crashing in the brush behind me, and then lost consciousness.

When I regained my senses, Don Jones was dumping me off the end of a pier into the bay. The frigid water quickly brought me around. After I dragged myself out and dried off with the rags that Don Jones handed me, he put me into my car and drove back to the farm. My body was on fire; I was covered with vivid red welts. Don Jones took me into his kitchen and covered me with a soothing pink lotion.

"I really flew, didn't I?" I asked as he ministered to me.

"Why ask me?" he replied. "You were there, weren't ye?"

"But how . . . ?"

"I think you know."

I thought so too, but I decided not to say anything.

A week later I had to return to the city, but Don Jones asked me to stay an additional day. There was something else he wanted to show me. At his request, I bought a gallon of muscatel to celebrate my departure.

As we sat on the front porch that evening, my mentor seemed unusually talkative, so I tried to ask about some of his teachings that I found puzzling.

"Don Jones," I asked, "What is the meaning of life?"

He lit his pipe and puffed in silence for a moment before he answered. "There are two sides of life, the left and the right," he answered. "The left hand never knows what the right hand is doin'. With perfect attention, you can lift the veil of the world and know what both hands're doin' at the same time." He took a long drink from the bottle. I told him I didn't understand what he was telling me.

"Oh, you understand, but ye don't *know* that ye understand. That's because ye can't see the veritable through the cracks in the world yet."

"What cracks," I asked.

Don Jones tipped the bottle up again. "The world is cracked. You saw the cracks that night in the potato field, and again when ye flew. The world's got a million cracks. Step on a crack, break yer mother's back." He drank the last of the muscatel, closed his eyes, and leaned back in his chair. In a moment I heard the soft rasp of his snoring.

I was frustrated and confused. I had spent months studying with this old man and had experienced things which I had thought impossible. Yet I felt no wiser. I shook Don Jones's shoulder to awaken him. Without warning his right hand snaked out and smacked me in the nose. Before I could move, his left caught me soundly behind the ear and sent me sprawling across the porch. "See what I mean?" he said.

"Don Jones, what are we going to do tomorrow?" I demanded.

"Transformations," he said. "Someone who *knows* the cracks in the world can touch the spirits of other creatures and transform himself into them. You'll see tomorrow. Now shut up and let me get some sleep."

Don Jones was snoring again in less than a minute. I was wide awake and strangely unsettled. I had the uncomfortable sensation that someone or something was tugging on my leg. Nothing seemed to make sense. I despaired about the months of fruitless work and study. I paced back and forth in my stall in the barn for hours before I could finally fall asleep.

The next morning, Don Jones told me to put on my rubber boots, because we were going down to the bay. We drove to a rocky promontory, parked, and walked out on boulders still wet from the receding tide. Don Jones began searching among the tidepools, stooping occasionally to lift a stone or turn over a clump of seaweed. I sat down on a dry rock and watched.

After a few moments, Don Jones found what he was looking for. He motioned for me to join him at the edge of a large tidepool. He held up a handful of seaweed--a variety I had never seen before. He tore off a small piece and chewed it, indicating that I should do the same.

As I chewed, that strange and by now all too familiar sensation I had first experienced in the potato field began to return. I stopped chewing and spit out the noxious mouthful. Almost immediately I experienced an amazing clarity of consciousness.

Don Jones was laughing and splashing around in the tidepool excitedly. He asked me if I was ready to witness a transformation. Reluctantly, I agreed.

Don Jones instructed me to look for more of the strange seaweed. I knelt by the edge of the tidepool and began my search. It took several moments to locate the plant and dislodge it from the rocks. When I turned back to hand it to him, Don Jones was no longer there. In the place where he had stood was the largest lobster I had ever seen.

It was delicious, too.

Things Could Be Worse

Yes, the news is endlessly discouraging. And it's been bad for quite a while. U.S. soldiers are dying in distant lands; we wonder when the next terrorist attack on our own soil may come. Too many of us are out of work. The federal deficit is exploding. Medical costs are spiraling upward. The Earth's climate is still warming. We're threatened by mad cows and pigs with the flu.

Still, things *could* be worse...

Chocolate May Cause Cancer, Study Suggests

Researchers at the National Institute of Health today disclosed the results of animal studies that indicate chocolate consumption may encourage the development of cancerous tumors in the digestive system. "Our findings are preliminary at this point," Dr. Arvid Patel said, "but I would recommend extreme caution to anyone partaking of this popular snack."

In Patel's study, mice fed a diet of chocolate covered food pellets were three times more likely to develop tumors than mice that were fed plain pellets, although they also seemed to anticipate feeding time much more enthusiastically than the control group. The chocolate-fed mice were also twenty-two percent heavier at the conclusion of the experiment...

Adam Sandler Cloned

Doctors at Beverly Hills Women's Hospital announced today they have successfully produced cloned offspring using DNA from epithelial cells obtained from Adam Sandler's cheek. Doctors removed the nuclear material from one hundred donated human egg cells, replaced it with Sandler's DNA, and implanted the eggs in one hundred volunteer surrogate mothers. Eighty-seven of those women eventually gave birth to apparently healthy babies. The children—now three years old--are being raised in an undisclosed location somewhere in the Los Angeles area. . .

Canadian Troops Massing Along The Border

Satellite surveillance indicates large concentrations of Canadian troops and equipment at two staging areas less than forty miles from the Canadian border with Michigan and New York State. Pentagon officials said the encampments include approximately 50,000 troops, as well as tanks, artillery and mobile rocket launchers. The Canadian Prime Minister characterized the deployment as purely defensive in nature. "As long as the United States respects the sovereign integrity of the world's other nations," he said, "its citizens have nothing to fear from Canadian forces." . . .

Chinese Restaurants To Close Worldwide

You may have eaten your last bowl of hot and sour soup. All Chinese restaurants outside the People's Republic will close their doors permanently on Friday. Many will reopen next month as insurance agencies, legal clinics or mattress stores. The closures are designed to place ethnic Chinese workers in higher-paying jobs, while simultaneously encouraging increased tourism to China itself. "Next week there will be only one place to get General Tso's chicken or mu shu pork," economic minister Yang Zedong announced. "We'll see you in Beijing." . . .

Two Days Added To February

Adjusting a calendar out of sync with the modern world, the U.S. Bureau of Standards today added two more days to the month of February. To maintain a calendar of 365 days, one day each was removed from May and August. "We recognize that this change may cause some distress," Wilton Moffatt, director of the agency said. "February is probably our least popular month, while May and August are generally regarded with fondness by the calendar-using public." Moffatt went on to discuss the need to rectify the inequity of restricting one month to only twenty-eight days while several others are allotted more than thirty. . .

***Won* Replaces U.S. Dollar as International Standard**

The world's leading banks today decided to replace the U.S. dollar with the South Korean *won* as the standard for currency exchange. The value of the *won* rose twenty-three percent on the news, while the dollar plummeted to record lows. "The dollar is no longer a reliable benchmark," Saudi economic minister Mahmoud Al-Jafr said. "Between the growing U.S. debt and continued trade deficits, we no longer consider it a stable currency. . . "

Shakespeare's Works Revealed as Hoax

The writings of "William Shakespeare," long revered as the greatest body of work in the English language, were confirmed yesterday as an elaborate deception perpetrated by a small, ingenious group of graduate students enrolled at Oxford University in the early 1800s. "We are quite embarrassed to make this disclosure public," University President Nigel Throckmorton confessed. "Student pranks are a longstanding tradition here at Oxford, but no one can recall one of quite this magnitude."

Worldwide, angry Shakespeare scholars expressed disbelief about the announcement. However, Throckmorton supported the revelation with reams of evidence recently unearthed in the back stacks of the university library. That evidence, now available on the internet, has set off a massive blizzard of new research into "the Bard's" works. . .

Nearby Star May Soon Explode As Supernova

Astronomers now suspect that slight fluctuations in the energy output of a nearby star may be the first indications that it is about to explode as a massive supernova. Betelgeuse, a type of star known as a red giant, is the right size and age to produce such a cataclysm. Because it is only 310 light years from earth, such an explosion could have devastating consequences on our own solar system.

Betelgeuse forms the eye of the constellation Taurus. It is one of the brightest stars in the night sky because of its proximity to earth. Dr. Sylvia Barton-Heinz of the Princeton Astronomical Institute points out that a supernova event might already have taken place. "Because of its distance, the first effects of the explosion would take more than three centuries to reach us. So at this very moment, an expanding shockwave of devastating electromagnetic force might already be on its way to destroy . . .

This piece was written well before the 2016 election. It even predates the 2000 Bush/Gore debacle and the years of endless war and the Great Recession that followed.

Apparently things could get <u>far</u> worse than I was able to imagine.

The Rock Garden Gone to Seed

By Sheldon Clamato

Newave Press, 107 pp.. $13.23

With this month's publication of *The Rock Garden Gone to Seed* by Newark native Sheldon Clamato, a new and revolutionary poetic voice has burst upon the literary scene.

In this slender volume, Clamato melds the two divergent strains of his Japanese-Jewish heritage into a fresh verse form which seems ideally suited to expressing the ironic incongruities of contemporary urban life. Here is an example from his series of poems on insomnia:

> The neighbors quarrel
>
> Their screams and accusations
>
> Pierce paper-thin walls.

Clamato calls his poetry "Lowku." In this new form, he has found a synthesis of the tingling sense of immediacy found in the traditional Japanese haiku and the overwhelming despair of the thoughtful urban dweller's misery in an age of decadence and waste.

Clamato's subjects cover the full range of our social and economic excesses. Yet his disturbing visions are expressed with the simple incisiveness of the traditional seventeen-syllable (more or less), three-line form. Writing Lowku is a spiritual discipline for Clamato, a means of coming to grips with the vast, conflicting forces buffeting modern humanity. In his verses, one can sense his intimate contact with the world around him, and the deep-seated revulsion he feels toward it. This should be apparent in the following three poems, chosen at random from *The Rock Garden Gone to Seed*.

>Asparagus fern
>
>Unwatered, broken and brown
>
>In a cracked clay pot.

>The white pustule swells
>
>And reddens into a huge lump
>
>On my nose. Acne.

>I pick up the soap.
>
>Clotted slime engulfs my hand.
>
>Faucet leaking again.

    Clamato can also show an occasional flash of humor hiding behind his world-weary and pessimistic view of technological society, as in this delightful poem, "Boogie Down."

> Snapping my fingers
>
> I dance down the aisles
>
> To the sound of Muzak.

Rock Garden is not without its faults. Clamato is frequently careless about line length in his poetry. The syllable counts in his Lowku range from as few as eleven to a high of twenty-nine. Some literary critics have found this carelessness inexcusable. Clamato responds by pointing out that as creator of the verse form, he can do whatever he damn well pleases with it. In fact, a certain sloppiness in the structure of the poems reinforces Clamato's thoughts about overflowing dumpsters, vinyl, rude waitresses, public toilets and hair in the sink.

But what of the apparent limitations of the Lowku form itself? A seventeen syllable poem would seem to make a poor vehicle for examining a complex industrial society in decay. In the hands of a lesser writer this would undoubtedly be so. However, in this one small volume Clamato has shown a master's ability to transcend the restrictions of his own chosen form, in which each word must be a carefully selected, glistening droplet of sludge.

Seventeen More Reasons to End the Arms Race

Sure, you know about plutonium, neutron bombs, overkill, and MIRVs. You've heard the arguments for and against the Nuclear Freeze and the "Starwars" anti-missile defense. You've even read Jonathan Schell's *The Fate of the Earth*. But you're still asking yourself, "What does this all have to do with *me*, personally?"

But arms control isn't just for the experts in Washington and Moscow. There are some very good reasons why Mr. and Mrs. Average Citizen should want to clamp a lid on the arms race, too. Like it or not, a global thermonuclear war will disrupt your personal life.

So, if you're one of those people who still think you'll be safer with an MX silo in your backyard and American H-bombs orbiting overhead, here are a few more reasons why we ought to stop the madness.

1. After a nuclear "exchange," there won't be enough people left to balance the federal budget and pay off the national debt, ever.

2. A nuclear war will ruin your portfolio of long-term investments, and make you feel like an idiot for squirreling all that money away in your IRA.

3. After the holocaust life insurance companies will have to pay off on one hundred million claims, all at once. Not to mention all those fire insurance settlements. There's

no way they'll be able to claim that a nuclear war was an "act of God," either. The companies will have to pay, and your premiums will go straight through the roof.

4. A "nuclear winter" will make it impossible to wear all those new summer fashions. Even worse, say goodbye to sitting around on the beach and watching lovely young people prance about in their colorful wisps of nylon.

5. After the nuclear winter is over, you'll want to work on your tan. Since the atmosphere's ozone layer will be gone, you'll be able to get a deep, tropical tan in just seconds. The trouble is, you won't be able to stay outside long enough for anyone else to admire it.

6. According to a recent poll, seven out of ten Americans believe they'll go to heaven when they die. But some modern theologians are troubled by the following question: Does the soul have time to leave the body when the body is vaporized in less than a millionth of a second? This enigma may trouble seven-tenths of the rest of us as well.

7. Your teenage daughter may be worried she'll miss the chance to experience the joys of love, because her life is about to be cut short by a blast of nuclear fire. Maybe she won't get pregnant if she and her ratty boyfriend don't think they have to do it quick, before the bombs fall.

8. Your kids already think that you and the other members of our generation are a bunch of screw-ups. Imagine what they'll think if we blow up the planet.

9. If we keep stockpiling bombs and missiles, we're going to run out of places to store surplus cheese. Federal

agents may have already measured your garage for this purpose, on the pretext of reading your gas meter or selling aluminum siding. Think of what the pervasive scent of cheddar will do to property values in your neighborhood.

10. Radiation makes your hair fall out. Many of us are going bald too quickly as it is.

11. The electromagnetic pulse from any nearby nuclear blast will blow out all the circuits in your brand new home computer, and erase your hard drive and all your old cassette tapes.

12. We've been broadcasting soap operas out into space for 30 years. Dozens of distant solar systems are now within range of *The Young and the Restless.* There's no telling how many alien cultures are now hooked on love in the afternoon. They would be devastated if a nuclear holocaust cut off their daily dose of the soaps.

12. Remember that dream trip you've been planning to the capitals of Europe? If we wipe Europe off the map, the vacation is off.

14. There isn't enough newsprint and ink available for newspapers to run all the obituaries a nuclear war would require. Fiscally and physically unable to meet their journalistic responsibilities, many daily papers would simply have to go out of business.

15. If you glow in the dark, it's going to be tougher sneaking into bed after a late night out with your buddies.

16. You know that guy at work who nags you to sign

petitions, go to rallies and donate money for the Nuclear Freeze? Wouldn't you just love for him to shut up and leave you alone for a while?

17. The 80's have already given us so much: New Coke, music videos, Louis Farrakhan, light beer, Miami Vice, Pia Zadora, 9-digit zip codes, Prince, and even a B-movie president.   Don't you want to find out what's next?

There. If that doesn't convince you, then I don't know what will.

Very few people want to read or think about the nuclear arms race—a fact made plain to me repeatedly over the years whenever I tried writing seriously about nuclear weapons issues. My second book, <u>Understanding the Vocabulary of the Nuclear Arms Race</u>, sold fewer than a thousand copies, despite receiving a starred review in School Library Journal.

[How's that for a catchy title? The editor's choice, not mine. I wanted to call it <u>A is for Atom, B is for Bomb</u>]

So, this was an (admittedly lame) attempt to come at it from a humorous angle, in the hope that readers might consider nuclear disarmament if they could laugh about it.
Oh, well.

Khomeini Ways Can You Say Ghotbzadeh?

The Iranian turmoil of recent months has generated huge difficulties for America. Our diplomats are held captive in a foreign land. We have been forced to reassess our role in world affairs. New scenarios have been written and rewritten in the paneled offices of the State Department, and new contingency plans drafted at the Pentagon. American citizens have found a renewed need to stand together in solidarity, after a decade of jogging, hot tubs and assertiveness training. None of this has been easy.

In addition, the crisis has also created difficulties of a less momentous nature. For example, just what should a patriotic American's attitude be toward Persian rugs or pistachio nuts?

But of all the minor aftershocks of the Iranian crisis, perhaps the one that has weighed most heavily on the American populace is the current disaster in broadcast journalism. Many an American newscaster has been left with his tongue tied securely around a bicuspid after attempting to read a dispatch from Tehran. Either the phonemes of Farsi are so foreign to American ears that they are virtually unpronounceable, or none of our electronic journalists have taken the trouble to ask an Iranian for proper pronunciations.

The problems of pronunciation, like so many other of our difficulties, seemed to begin with that diabolical prophet, the Ayatollah. When he first rose to prominence, broadcasters, variously pronounced his name as HO-may-nee, KO-may-nee, ho-may-NEE, ko-may-NEE, ho-MAY-nee and ko-MAY-nee. No one seemed able to identify that elusive accented syllable.

After long months of news reports, the last two pronunciations seem to have won out. Incidentally, Walter Cronkite, our most respected video journalist, seems to favor ho-MAY-nee. Unfortunately, we have no way of knowing whether Mr. Cronkite's is the definitive pronunciation, or merely the one that he has found to be the most personally agreeable.

Iran's current president has also caused problems for broadcasters. Everyone seems to agree on the first portion of the name. They pronounce it as if it came right out of that old Scottish tune, "My Bani lies over the ocean." However, the terminal *dr* is unfamiliar to English-speaking tongues. Consequently, we have heard BAH-nee SOD-ruh, BAH-nee SOD-ur, BAH-nee sah-DAHR, and even BAH-nee SOD.

On one recent evening, CBS correspondent Bernard Kalb pronounced the name as SOD-ruh, while anchorman Cronkite pronounced it SOD-ur. Should we trust the man in the field, who should be in the best position to know, or the respected anchorman, who should make it his business to know?

More recently, correspondent Tom Fenton began a report with the pronunciation SOD-rrrrr with a classic rolled *r*. He then switched to SOD-ur for his second reading of the name, and finally ended his report with a simple BAH-nee

SOD.

But American reporters have suffered their worst trials in attempting to pronounce the name of Iran's current foreign minister. We have heard at least as many different pronunciations of that name as there are newscasters. The minister, the central figure in months of news reports, has had his name pronounced as HOPE-sa-day, GOPES-a-day, GOPE-za-dee, GOPE-suh-duh, GOATS-bah-day, GUP-tza-day, GOATS-buh-ZAH-duh, and even goat-BOOZ-a-day. And who knows--perhaps *none* of those is correct.

Each report seemed to bring a new pronunciation. Often we have heard reporters using two or three different pronunciations within the space of a single ninety-second report.

Surely there is one correct pronunciation of the name, and surely some reporter has taken the trouble to find it. But which reporter? How can we know who among all those distinguished and highly-paid journalists has taken the time to find out how the name should be pronounced, and then trained his recalcitrant tongue to pronounce it that way?

Lately, reporters have been trying to find a way around the worst of the Iranian pronunciation crisis. The strategy has *Ghotbzadeh* appearing less and less frequently in their news reports. The reporters have discovered that if the man is not mentioned in their dispatches, they need not attempt a pronunciation. When it becomes impossible to avoid mentioning Ghotbzadeh, the journalists have taken to tackling the name only once, at the beginning of their report. For the remainder of their account, he is referred to as "the foreign minister," or "the Iranian spokesman."

Undoubtedly, resolution of the Iranian crisis will bring a great collective sigh of relief from our nation. Perhaps only the hostages and their families will feel a greater sense of deliverance than our perplexed and harried broadcasters. After months of lingual trauma, what bliss to once again inform us of events with principals named Menachim Begin, Valery Giscard d'Estaing and Deng Xiaoping.

This piece may be a bit dated, but similar problems still dog the news media. Even the highly respected reporters from NPR aren't immune. Their newsreaders can't seem to agree on how to pronounce the name of <u>one of their own correspondents</u>! We've recently heard a series of excellent, detailed reports from Leila Fadel in Cairo. (spelling from the NPR web site.) Most NPR news anchors pronounce her name as "Foddle." However, in her own reports, she always signs off as Leila "Fall-din." One would suspect she knows how to pronounce her own name—but the other news readers just haven't caught on.

A Dreadful Green Shade of Purple

I had just finished scrubbing the foredeck of the Flushed Buzzard when the ship's alarm told me I had a visitor. The Buzzard is an old garbage scow I won on a bet a few years back. I spent a couple of days cleaning her up and now I live on her year round. It's a little primitive, but it beats the heck out of what passes for life in those expensive high-rise apartments on the beach. No insurance salesmen, no frozen TV dinners, no midnight noises through the walls, no running water.

Where was I? Oh, yes. I slipped aft to greet my guest. She was the kind of visitor I'd welcome aboard anytime. Honeyed skin, firm breasts, and the wide-set eyes you see in fashion magazines. She smiled tentatively. Beneath the outer radiance I could sense a festering shadow.

"Mr. McBee?" she asked. Her lower lip quivered.

"Welcome to Trampas McBee's floating pleasure palace," I said.

Suddenly the dam burst. "Oh, Mr. McBee, I didn't think I'd find you," she sobbed. "Roger told me to come if I ever needed help."

I knew who she was then. Roger Wiley's young widow, Jennifer. Roger and I had been fishing buddies. One year a hurricane hit while we were down in the Keys. Three days of fighting for survival against the winds and tide can build a friendship fast—or break one.

Later he started a little maritime shipping firm that grew big. He invited me to go in with him but I turned him down. We've only got a little time on this planet. Why tie yourself down with the endless struggle to make money, just to end up too old and decrepit to spend any of it? I guess I've just seen too many... Hunh? Oh, sorry.

Anyway, Roger married a woman twenty years younger than he was, and died of a heart attack two months later. And now she was aboard my boat, sobbing on my shoulder.

I finally got the story out of her. It was all too familiar.

Roger had done well in some ways that were not quite legal. In addition to his legitimate operations, he had earned a tidy income smuggling real estate. Just before he died, he gave Jennifer a sealed shoebox and told her to hide it under the bed for an emergency.

Then two weeks ago she met a young man with big muscles and tousled blond hair. It was her first time since Roger's death, and she fell hard. A week later he was gone, and so was the box.

"What was in the box, Mrs. Wiley?"

"Oh, I don't know. Jewels, money. You know, valuable stuff."

"Did you ever open it?"

"No. I trusted Roger completely." The sobbing began again.

"Sorry," I told her. "I don't think I can help you."

"But you're my only hope."

"I just made a big recovery. I have enough money stashed to last me for the next three weeks."

It was as if somebody just flipped a switch. A sultry look appeared in her eyes, "I can make it worth your while, McBee." She unbuttoned the top two buttons of her filmy yellow blouse.

"Jenny, if you're not careful, you'll catch cold."

"Keep me warm then, McBee," she purred.

Her eager fingers tugged at my belt buckle. Sure, McBee. Play the knight on the white steed. It will make you feel self-righteous as hell. What does it matter? We'll all be grinning in our plush-lined caskets before too long. Why not admit that you're no different from any other . . .

"McBee?"

"Yeah?"

"Nothing. I just had the feeling your mind was somewhere else."

A long, sweet time later, I explained how I worked. "I steal back things people lose. It's risky, so I get paid well for it. If I get your shoebox back, you get ten percent. I also get to take a girl on a cruise afterwards. If you're still alive, it'll probably be you."

"Ninety percent seems kind of steep."

"You can't go to the cops. Roger was a smuggler. Take it or leave it."

"You're a real bastard, McBee. I'll take it."

I asked my old-friend Feinstein to keep an eye on Jennifer while I tried to make a few bucks from the mess she'd made of her life. Good old Feinstein. Ten years ago he retired from a successful embezzling career. He bought himself a nice little boat, the Queen Mary, and tied her up across from my scow. I've depended on him for help and advice ever since.

We have a great arrangement. He invests my money for a neat twenty percent per week, and I let him hang around my boat, leering at my little WASP cuties. Feinstein was already drooling over Jennifer when I left.

It didn't take long to track down Jennifer's friend. He was registered at one of the new motels just outside of town. What are architects thinking when they design one of these concrete tombs? Everything seems deliberately cold and repulsive. They camouflage it with carpet, cheap paintings and welcome signs, but they can't hide the inhuman hardness underneath. How can anyone relax in ... Oh, damn. Give me another chance. I'll stick to the story, I promise.

I got the room number from the desk clerk.

"He's a popular guy," the scrawny, pimply-faced young man behind the desk told me. "You're the second one's asked about him tonight."

A cold shiver crawled up my spine, and a subconscious warning gnawed at my brain. I went into the lounge and drank until it went away.

Half an hour later I walked down the corridor and knocked on number 143. No one said "come in," so I tried the doorknob. The door swung open. The man I was looking for was sprawled peacefully across the bed.

"Let's have the box," I said calmly. No answer.

"It belongs to the lady," I said. I was about to get angry when I noticed that his tousled blond head was lying at an unnatural angle in the bottom bureau drawer. The rest of him lay quietly across the bloodstained covers. His lips were curled in a horrid grin and his face was a dreadful green shade of purple.

Suddenly I felt a sharp stinging sensation at the back of my neck, and I was rolling across the floor. I sat up and peered at my attacker through a haze of pain.

"I want what's in that box," he barked.

"I don't have any box."

"Don't give me that." He came at me. He had the arms and shoulders of a grizzly. I wasn't sure I could handle him.

He reared back and swung at me. I grabbed for his crutch as it whistled past my ear and got a bruised left hand for the effort.

He drew back for a second swing. Unless I moved fast, it would be the last. I dove for his spindly legs, and we both went sprawling. I caught a vicious, slashing blow from one of his leg braces as we went down.

I made a desperate grab for the wooden crutch. I

wrenched it from his grasp and swung. There was a sickening crunch, like someone dropping a ripe watermelon. My attacker twitched once and lay still.

Finding the box was easy. It was in the bottom dresser drawer beside the head, unopened, hidden under several gray undershirts.

Now all that was left was to deal with the deputy sheriff. There's always a deputy involved in these recoveries, and he's either crooked or stupid. I sat down and waited.

He showed up ten minutes later. I didn't get his name. The tag above his breast pocket was pinned on upside down. A stupid one. "What's going on here?" he growled.

"A birthday party. For you. Surprise!"

"Lucky guess, McBee, but not lucky enough. My birthday ain't till next Tuesday."

He looked around the room. "You got a problem, McBee. It's gonna cost to keep this quiet." Stupid *and* crooked.

"How much?"

"Fifty, at least"

I pulled a hundred out of my wallet. "Keep the change. Get yourself a lobotomy."

"Gee, thanks, McBee." I picked up the shoebox and started for the door. Sometimes this business is just too easy. I kicked him in the knee on my way out.

When I got back to the *Buzzard*, Feinstein was snoring

on my bunk and Jennifer was getting ready to fry some eggs. I caught her hand just as she was about to spray the pan with one of those aerosol oil substitutes.

She gasped and stared at me. We're so hooked on our spray-on conveniences we've forgotten what reality is like. We spray away odor, spray our hair into place, spray away any nasty bug that wants to spoil our picnic. We'll spray away the ozone layer, even if it means we'll all die of skin cancer. .. What? I'm sorry. One more chance, please?

She opened the shoebox. Inside were the few pieces of paper at least two men had died for. Three hundred thousand in negotiable securities, and a dozen polaroid shots of a very well-known politician in the company of a very naked woman.

"I'll make sure these won't do any more harm," I told her, carefully slipping the photos into my pocket.

"Was it rough, McBee?" Jennifer looked at the purple bruise on my neck and the crusted blood on my shirt.

"Nothing a quiet cruise with plenty of sex won't cure." I riffled the securities. "As soon as I cash these in we'll be on our way."

"We? What if I don't want to go?"

"That was part of the deal, remember?"

And then she flipped that switch again. "I guess we better make the most of it," she purred. She loosened the belt on her flimsy nylon gown and pressed close to me. I put my hands around her waist. I wonder if anyone even remembers what natural silk feels like anymore. Everything is wash-and-wear, drip-dry synthetics now. Chemical companies strip millions of acres of trees so that we can all wear slinky artificial clothes that won't even absorb honest sweat. What will we wear when all the trees are gone? If we're lucky, someone will have squirreled away a few cotton seeds. . . Oh, damn! I didn't mean it, Lew. I try to control myself but... What do you mean, "no cruise and no girl?"

Hey, put that gun away! Look, Mr. Archer, one more chance, please. Please! No!

John D. MacDonald told a good story—albeit a formulaic one. His series of Travis McGee thrillers were a guilty pleasure of mine. And he loved to have his detective pontificate on the failures of modern American life.

And of course, there was Ross Macdonald, a master of the hard-boiled detective story. Lew Archer, his protagonist, had to untangle complex mysteries with a long backstory. If you're a fan of detective fiction, he's a writer to be savored.

Newly Discovered Work by Tolkien Published

The Houghton-Mifflin Publishing Company today released the first copies of the late J. R. R. Tolkien's 700 page *Tarandoth Os Mifildar*, which had been discovered last April by lawyers responsible for the author's estate. Orders from booksellers throughout the world have already exceeded the 100,000-copy first printing, despite the fact that the entire work is written in an as yet undeciphered language devised by Tolkien himself.

Apparently the author never found the time to complete a dictionary of the language. In any case, no glossary or key has been found among his papers. Thus *Tarandoth Os Mifildar* remains, at least for the time being, totally unintelligible.

Nevertheless, the massive volume appears destined to be an instant best-seller. This is due for the most part to the enormous worldwide popularity Tolkien's other works enjoy. However, critics who received advance copies of the new work are already praising the discovery on its own merits. One noted critic has called *Tarandoth Os Mifildar* a "lyrical work of mystic and mysterious poetry." Another has proclaimed Tolkien a "genius whose mastery of the written word transcends mere meaning."

One can sense this linguistic expertise in the following brief passage, excerpted from what appears to be the fourth chapter.

Harton os banir. Na me tofarron laduna kwa misochin. Ildinfur arten bot vooris Mislindar sora retendo. Barnoost Arillden os waadin kwa baalankor do islindar baraak, twoldur mirnath neb hanaffil seng doth.

In an effort to decipher *Tarandoth Os Mifildar*, Houghton-Mifflin has assembled some the world's best cryptographers and instructed them to translate the book into English, no matter how long it may take. The publishing house has put the latest high-speed computers at these experts' disposal, but thus far little progress has been made. In the meantime, thousands of readers will soon be delighting in the sonorous, albeit incomprehensible prose of one of the past century's best-loved authors.

This short piece was originally published in <u>Write Now!</u>, a collection of original classroom writing activities. I'm not sure why the editor agreed to include it—even though I requested it—as it had <u>absolutely</u> <u>nothing</u> to do with the rest of the book. I did appreciate the gesture though.

So You Think You Have Tax Problems...

Internal Revenue Service, Western Regional Office

San Francisco, California

Mr. K. Midas:

Sutter's Mill Parkway

Eureka, California

Dear Mr. Midas,

Several irregularities in your 1985 tax return have been brought to my attention by the auditors in my department. Because of the highly unusual nature of the 1040 form you filed with us, we must ask you to appear at our offices on May 17, 1987 with a complete set of your financial records for the year in question.

So that you will be able to reply to our inquiries fully, I would like to inform you of the nature of the irregularities we have found. I hope this will be helpful as you prepare to meet with us in May.

First, as you surely know, your return was filed on a sheet of heavy gold leaf that appears to be an exact replica of our Form 1040. Federal law requires that all tax returns must be filed on standard IRS forms. You certainly must appreciate that the use of non-standard forms makes it impossible for our computers to process returns accurately and efficiently. I hope that this unusual method of filing does not signify an uncooperative attitude towards the IRS. We would look upon such behavior with great disfavor.

In addition, examination of your return shows several responses that are not acceptable for tax computation purposes. In particular, on line 31, which asks for adjusted gross income, the response "unlimited" cannot be used to compute a final tax figure. Nor can we accept without further clarification the exemption that you claim for a solid gold statue of your daughter, or your $8,500 deduction for jewelry polish. Finally there is the matter of payment of your tax liabilities. You indicated that payment was to accompany your return. We have yet to receive it, although the Postal Service is currently holding several large, heavy packages they have been unable to deliver to us due to insufficient postage.

I'm sure that when we meet in May these matters can be clarified and your 1985 return can be properly submitted and cleared. I'm eagerly awaiting the opportunity to shake your hand and to hear an explanation of your most unusual tax situation.

Ours truly,

William Greene, Senior Auditor

This piece also first appeared in <u>Write Now</u>! Again, I'm not sure why, but thanks.

Two All-Beef Patties, Special Delivery

There it was, the familiar red sign with the golden arches. They're yellow, really, Nick Lundsberg thought. Calling them "golden" was a nice touch, but then you don't sell billions of burgers without having plenty of smarts.

He checked the clock on the dashboard. 12:15. Forty-five minutes to grab a bite before he had to get to his next appointment.

Nick slipped past the yellow traffic light and turned into the parking lot. The drive-thru line was surprisingly long, stretching completely around the restaurant, so he decided to park and walk inside. That way he'd have a chance to wash up and take a leak, too.

Something seemed different to Nick when he walked through the glass entryway into the restaurant. Still, he didn't give it much thought until after his trip to the restroom. Then it hit him. Instead of the usual three or four short service lines, there was one long one. And there was only one worker behind the counter, at that moment filling a white paper bag with someone's order. She was wearing an unusual uniform, too--a gray shirt with a little red, white and blue eagle sewn over the pocket.

They're trying something different, Nick thought. Leave it to McDonald's to find the most efficient way to do everything. If only Metropolitan Mechanical would develop a similar attitude, he might be able to spend a little more time in the office, and a little less driving around from one customer to another.

Nick noticed that the line hadn't seemed to move much. Strange, he thought. Meanwhile, three other people had gotten in line behind him. The guy ahead of Nick, apparently a construction worker on his lunch break, turned around and shrugged.

"What's going on?" Nick asked. "Any idea what the hold-up is?"

"No idea," the man said, "but I've about had it. I have to get back to work in fifteen minutes."

"Don't you guys read the newspaper?" a voice behind them said.

Nick turned around. A stout man wearing a plaid jacket looked at him incredulously.

"You haven't heard about the nationalization?" Nick shook his head.

"Nationalization," the man repeated. "The U.S. Postal Service runs the American fast food industry now. They took over two weeks ago."

"Wait a minute," Nick said. "I think I heard something about that on the TV. Something to do with the national debt, right?"

The line inched forward, as the next customer stepped to the counter to be served.

Nick looked at his watch. 12:27.

"You got it," the man said. "To keep the country from going bankrupt, the government had to take over our most productive industry."

"But . . . that's socialism!"

"The president and the congress both agreed it was the only way. It was either that, or sell Hawaii to the Chinese." The line crept forward again.

"But why the Postal Service?"

"They were the ones in place. Every little town already had a postmaster who could be assigned to run the program."

The Post Office! The same people who had taken a week and a half to deliver a birthday card to his mother--on the other side of town. Nick had caught hell from her about it, too.

He shook his head in disbelief. The last time he had been in the Post Office, he had been forced to explain to the clerk what he wanted—twice—while the man fiddled with some sort of electronic entry on the counter. Then the clerk couldn't find an express mail stamp in his own stamp drawer.

Nick turned back around to check the progress of the line. The construction worker was just stepping up to the counter. Nick stood patiently beside a sign which read "Please wait for next available server..."

"I'd like a quarter pounder, a large fries and a ..."

"Just a moment," the server said sourly. "I can only fill

one order at a time. That's a quarter pounder?"

"Right."

The server carefully wrote something on a small pad of paper, tore it off, and turned around to the warming tray behind her. She checked what she had written on the paper, picked up a wrapped hamburger and put it in a white paper bag.

"Now, what else would you like?" she asked.

"I'd like to know where everybody else is," the man asked. "It's lunch time."

"That's right sir, it *is* lunch time," she replied coldly. "And most of our staff is *at lunch*. However, Mr. Harper is on the grill, and Ms. Neill is inventorying our French fries."

"Great. We certainly wouldn't want our restaurant employees to miss lunch, would we?"

"We're postal employees now, sir. We have a union contract. Do you want to order anything else?"

"A large Coke, please."

The server placed a paper cup under the fountain spout and pressed the Coke button. There was a brief gaseous eruption, then nothing. "Sorry, I seem to be out of Coke," she said.

"'What about those over there?" the construction worker asked, pointing to a second fountain further down the back counter.

"Sorry, that's not my station," was the reply. "How

about a diet root beer?"

"Never mind," the man said. He threw some money on the counter, picked up his hamburger and stalked through the door, muttering obscenities.

"Next please," the server announced. Nick approached the counter. The server scribbled something on another piece of paper--apparently some sort of daily report. Nick waited for her to look up and give him her attention. The clerk kept her attention firmly riveted to the form.

Finally Nick spoke up. "I'll have a Big Mac and a ..."

"Just a minute... She placed the form in a folder, and then placed the folder in a drawer beneath the counter. Then she looked up. "I'm sorry," she said, "this line is closed. If you step back for a moment, someone else will be out to help you."

Nick's frustration finally boiled to the surface. "Listen," he growled , "I've been waiting here for twenty minutes. I have an appointment to get to. This is supposed to be a *fast* food restaurant."

"I apologize if you're not satisfied with our service," the server answered. "If you'd like to file a complaint with the postmaster, I can give you our McCustomer McComplaint Form, CCF-273/A."

"I don't want a piece of paper. I want lunch! Let me talk to your manager."

"Our McManager is in Memphis for a training session, sir. But I can let you talk to her assistant."

She turned and walked into the kitchen area. A moment later a small, mousy-looking man with a thin moustache emerged. "I'm Mr. Harper. What seems to be the trouble, sir?" he asked.

"All I want is a Big Mac, French fries and a Coke." Nick said, "and to get out of here before next Thursday."

"I think we can take care of that." the man said. "Would you like that first class?"

"Special delivery. Just give me the damned hamburger."

The assistant manager turned and placed Nick's order in a paper bag. "That'll be fifteen dollars and seventy-five cents," he said as he put the bag on the counter.

"Fifteen seventy-five," Nick said, "for a burger, fries and a coke? Since when?"

"Our rates went up on Monday, sir. The Postmaster General granted us an increase. And we believe you'll begin to see improvements in the quality of our service almost immediately."

PBS Faces Reality

We hope you've enjoyed watching "Can't Hit the High Notes," with some of your favorite oldies groups. Remember, it's still pledge month on PBS. Please support your local PBS station by calling the number on your screen.

Meanwhile, tonight we have a *very* special announcement. Public Broadcasting has decided to capitulate. In the coming season, we too will be broadcasting our own unique assemblage of reality-based programming. What exciting new shows can you expect in the coming year? Just listen to this line-up.

Are You Smarter than a First Year Grad Student?

A team of contestants randomly selected from the studio audience will match wits with a panel of newly-matriculated graduate students from lesser-known universities. On our first program, three audience members square off against three first-year masters candidates from the English department at the University of Wyoming. Don't miss the fireworks as they interpret symbolic language in the works of English poet John Donne!

In following shows, panelists will examine ion transport across cell membranes in the neurons of the veined squid, *Loligo forbesii*; and analyze pottery fragments from archeological sites in Central America.

Grant or No Grant

Staff and board members of small non-profit organizations vie for money to fund their programs for the coming year.

In the first episode, four non-profits that provide after-school tutoring and recreational services to the children of migrant farm-workers must complete a twelve-page application for a $20,000 grant to help fund their operating expenses for the coming year. Tensions run high as board members struggle to clarify and reword their respective organizations' mission and vision statements.

Colonial Life

Follow the real-life, subterranean soap opera that takes place each day in a colony of black ants.

In the premier, a group of foraging workers face danger as they search for food on the limb of a sycamore tree. Meanwhile, there's trouble in the nursery—the larvae are demanding more and more attention. The queen has stopped laying eggs until the quality of her regurgitated food improves. And the winged males of the colony insist they be fed even though they refuse to do any useful work.

Survivor: Paris

Imagine subsisting in Paris—the most expensive city on earth--on only 500 Euros a day.

That's the challenge facing four young couples, each of whom meet one another for the very first time at the Tuilleries on a warm spring afternoon. Can they somehow find meals and lodging, and keep themselves entertained for a full week? Will romance or resentment bloom while they tackle an increasingly difficult series of obstacles? Their first task: find a *boulangerie*—or *bakery* as they say in France—that sells *tartes au pommes*. Will it be as difficult as it sounds?

Pundit Palace

Sure, they make it look effortless on The News Hour. But imagine how difficult it is to provide analysis and predictions at a moment's notice, day after day, on topics ranging from electoral politics to international relations to the global economy.

Which experts *really* know what they are talking about? To find out, we've leased a mansion in the northern Virginia suburbs, just outside the beltway. We'll invite ten political stargazers—faces viewers know all too well from their frequent appearances on *The News Hour*. Each week, we'll measure these pundits' predictions against the cold, hard truth of ensuing events. And each week, the pundit whose prognostications stray farthest from the news will be asked to depart. Ten sages move in to Pundit Palace, but in the end, only one will remain.

123 Sesame Street

The cameras aren't always rolling on Sesame Street. At least not until now.

When production shuts down for the day, beloved Sesame Street celebrities return to their off-screen lives at 123 Sesame Street. Now, for the first time, PBS cameras will follow them home for a peek into their private, off-screen lives.

What will Cookie Monster order when he and Grover go out for dinner after the show? Do Bert and Ernie *ever* stop arguing about whose turn it is to take out the garbage? How does Oscar handle the embarrassment when a group of fans mistake him for Elmo? And who would have suspected a bitter feud between Big Bird and Snuffleupagus that's lasted for more than a decade?

What you see on this new series may shock you. Believe us, it's not *always* a sunny day on Sesame Street.

Yes, things are going to get *even more real* on PBS this year. This is *your* television network. We understand the kind of programming *you* want to see. So enjoy our next two-hour presentation, "You Know This Already: Obvious Advice from a Self-appointed Financial Guru." And don't forget to call in that pledge!

Education

The Fun Subs Have

Last fall, having muddled through the generation gap, the energy crunch, and a protracted Constitutional crisis, I found myself facing a new, more personal difficulty. I was a *bona fide*, certified teacher, but my unemployment rate was 100 percent. Since I was thoroughly trained as an educator, at great expense to my parents and the federal government, and not particularly handy with hammers, backhoes or balance sheets, I decided to pursue my calling as best I could. I signed up to become a substitute teacher.

Of course, substituting runs a poor second to watching your own class develop into great thinkers, thanks to your creative and resourceful teaching. But it is *almost* teaching, and I did learn a few things I would like to share with my colleagues in the classroom and on the unemployment line.

First of all, I've found that being a substitute, or "subbing" as we say in the ed biz, places me in a strange moral position. I wake up early each morning hoping someone else is sick. My economic well-being depends on a fellow teacher's ill health. Things only get worse if I extend this line of reasoning further: If someone gets seriously ill, I might get a long-term position, with a chance to do some "real" teaching. And if I get really lucky and someone dies, I might be considered for a full-time position! All this begins to conjure up visions of Beelzebub appearing in a sulfurous cloud to strike his bargain: my immortal soul for a fifth grade classroom.

Nor do things improve when I am finally established in my school for the day. I am immediately faced with another crisis. Inevitably some good-natured teacher will come up to me and ask, in all earnestness, "Well, who are you today?" So much for my personal identity. This existential query calls for a different response each day. Sometimes the best answer I can come up with is "You know the reading teacher down the hall? I think her name begins with an R."

It isn't an easy task for a sub to maintain mental balance. Remember your first day as a teacher? For a substitute, *every* day is the first day, with new school procedures, new subject matter, and new, often hostile faces. A sub is endlessly establishing rapport and learning bell schedules. On good days, the challenge can be rather exciting, but sometimes I feel as though I were somewhere in the Minoan maze without my ball of string.

Then there are the students. I've come to suspect that a great majority of them are less than devoted to the pursuit of knowledge. When I arrive they are suddenly plagued with stomachaches, headaches, toothaches and more mysterious maladies, all of which seem to require passes to the nurse. They suffer unaccountable losses of memory concerning studies of the previous day. They tell wild tales of libertine teachers who "let them" do anything from completing math homework during English to playing a bit of touch football in place of completing a history assignment. And they are amazingly busy, with counselors to see, errands to run and reports to write in the library, all of which must be accomplished during my class period.

A trusting substitute could begin writing passes for students' seemingly legitimate requests, only to look up from the desk several minutes later to find the last four students remaining in the classroom all sound asleep.

There's no doubt students often try to take advantage of substitute teachers--and they often succeed. Some make a game of seeing how much they can get away with, how much anger, outrage or embarrassment they can elicit. They treat substitutes to an endless parade of attention-seeking behaviors. Sometimes four-letter words hover in the air like bats' cries, just beyond human hearing.

Meanwhile the substitute has to maintain a calm, relaxed, good-humored attitude--and at the same time insist on an acceptable level of quiet and effort. This can be a difficult compromise to reach in the face of apathetic or ornery students and skimpy lesson plans. If I were to make an issue out of every outburst by an ill-mannered student, I would find myself in a constant battle that would probably end with my peace of mind among the casualties.

On the other hand, I need to retain my livelihood. If my adopted class can be heard as far away as the main office, I probably won't be invited back again. A substitute must tread the razor's edge between sanity and unemployment.

My greatest delight as a substitute has been the few

times when a class has arrived and gotten down to work on their own, as if I weren't even there. At these times I feel that I'm witnessing some evidence of genuine education, as opposed to "schooling." I always try to write a note complimenting the teachers of these rare classes for helping their students get excited about learning and then allowing them to satisfy their aroused curiosities--and for preparing them in advance for the inevitable day when their teacher will be absent.

But when the lesson plan reads something vague like "continue with long division," and the kids are getting restless, I sometimes fall back on an educational game or song that will involve the whole class. Generally, even unruly students will see that something good is happening and generate enough self-discipline to participate in the class activity.

I've been amused to discover that games popular with elementary pupils can also generate excitement among older students. I feel more hope for the future after watching big arrogant seniors losing themselves in a quick round of 20 questions. I never walk into a classroom without a few little goodies in mind from that bag of tricks, in case things start to fall apart. It's like having an ace reliever in the bullpen.

Classroom teachers may wonder just how effective their efforts to instill a love of their subject matter have been, or how well their students have internalized their behavior management system, or what they say behind the teachers' backs. The substitute probably knows. Students' behavior and comments on days when the teacher is absent could be useful as feedback for evaluating teacher effectiveness.

The sub might be able to help a teacher find out just how genuine their interest in the subject matter truly is. Have they really enjoyed studying the War of 1812 for six weeks, or are they just trying to be polite? But teachers, don't ask unless you really want to know. From what this substitute has seen, the War of 1812 probably captivates them much less than you think.

It is a basic tenet of the American ethic that struggle in the face of adversity builds character. If this is so, our nation has a great reservoir of fortitude in its unheralded legions of substitute teachers. The job's financial rewards are matched only by its status in the educational hierarchy and the solid satisfaction of working with students for a day or two and then never seeing them again.

So teachers, when you return to class after a well-deserved illness to discover your plans are disrupted, the students are undisciplined, and the room is littered with paper wads, do try to find a charitable thought. If nothing else, think about how much fun your substitute must have had.

Today's Education (The NEA Journal), Nov. 1976

This essay was the very first piece of writing I ever "sold" to a national publication.

I didn't actually get paid for it. But it did go out to more than a million NEA members. And I suspect it was a contributing factor in my being hired by Richmond Public

Schools a couple of years later—and so helped me find my way to a 27-year teaching position—one that gave me the opportunity to create innovative lesson plans, collaborate with a terrific group of colleagues, and spend many, many hours with wonderful, bright, motivated and creative elementary and middle school students.

The Reading Teacher at Work:
A Revealing Glimpse for Parents

Of course, today's parents are concerned about what is being taught to their children at school, and *how* it is being taught. Rightly so. Parents should keep abreast of the latest developments in pedagogy.

Reading is undoubtedly the most critical skill taught in the elementary grades. For educators who want to give parents and other concerned citizens an idea of how the first R is being taught in the modern classroom, we here excerpt a complete reading lesson from the teachers' edition of *Gossamer Wings and Other Things*, the third-grade reader published by Lern-Rite Press of Chicago. The lesson below is typical of instructional material available to reading teachers today.

Little Red Riding Hood

Objectives: After reading and discussing Lesson 7, the student will

--Demonstrate an empathetic understanding for victims of violent crime in our society.

--Make appropriate judgements about the unsafe and foolhardy behavior practiced by the ingenuous heroine of the story.

--Discuss the advantages and disadvantages of expending vast amounts of federal money to protect an endangered species.

--Given a list of animals, correctly categorize them as predator, prey, or both, with 80% accuracy.

Story Synopsis: A young girl carrying a basket of goodies to her grandmother meets a big bad wolf in the forest. The wolf rushes to grandmother's house, devours the old woman, gristle and all, and takes her place in bed. Disguised as the grandmother, he tricks Red Riding Hood and is about to have his way with her (and eat her too) when a woodsman walks by. Hearing the commotion, he bludgeons the wolf to death with his axe.

Suggestions for Teaching: First introduce students to the new vocabulary words. Then have them read the story silently, preferably in a darkened room. Most students should be able to read the entire story independently in one sitting. Follow up with Questions for Discussion and the Skills Lesson. Advanced students may be assigned one or more of the Enrichment Activities.

Vocabulary: fang, drooling, mangy, lupine, opportunistic, hood, goodies, tasty, curvaceous, leer, bludgeon.

Questions for Discussion:

—What do you think Red had in the basket? How might your ideas change if you knew Grandma had no teeth?

—How do you think Red got her name? Do you know any other children named after items of clothing?

—How do you think Red felt when she first met the wolf? Why didn't he eat Red then and there?

—Why did the wolf eat Grandma even though she was tough and stringy?

—When she first got to the house, Red thought that the wolf was her Grandmother. This probably happened because

    a. Red was myopic.

    b. Red was extremely gullible.

    c. Red had an extremely ugly grandmother

—The woodsman came along to save Red just in the nick of time because

    a. He was guided by the Divine Hand of Providence.

    b. Red's being eaten would have made a messy ending for the story.

    c. He was in the woods looking for little girls himself.

—What happened to the wolf at the end of the story? Provide plenty of gory details.

—Imagine you are a member of the Women's Liberation Front. What would your position be on the story of Little Red Riding Hood?

Skills Lesson: Duplicate the following lists and distribute a copy to each student. Explain the concepts of "predator" and "prey" to the class. Then have each student match each predator with the prey it typically pursues.

Crocodiles	Flies
Dogs	Swimmers
Spiders	Garbage
Rats	Billy Goats Gruff
White whales	Captains' hands
Trolls	Captains' legs
Humans	Table scraps
White Sharks	Cows, pigs, sheep, goats, ducks, chickens, turkeys, geese, deer, turtles, fish, frogs, snakes, chocolate- covered ants

Enrichment Activities:

1. (Dramatics) Have selected students dramatize the story for the rest of the class. The role of the wolf is particularly appropriate for a child with behavioral control issues.

2. (Science/Math) Give each child a metric ruler and a wolf. Have them measure the size of fangs, claws and other body parts to the nearest centimeter.

3. (Health and Safety) Have students make posters depicting safety rules for delivering baskets of goodies through dark wooded areas.

4. (Social Studies/Environmental Science) The wolf is considered an endangered species. This is due in part to the sharp decline in Red Riding Hoods, a staple of their diet.

Have students draw pictures and write reports about other endangered species.

5. (Physical Education) Fill a large burlap sack with sawdust. Give the students axe handles, baseball bats, blackjacks and other blunt instruments. Then play a game of "Bludgeon the Wolf. The first child to make sawdust run from the sack is the winner.

Phi Delta Kappan, April 1978

May I Have Your Attention, Please

Remember that intercom high up on the classroom wall above your teacher's desk? Maybe you called it a "PA", short for public address system. Well, it's still there. I know, because I have one in my classroom, and after 15 years of teaching it's still driving me crazy.

I've worked in several different schools. They've all had intercoms, with a level of acoustical fidelity just one step above a tin-can telephone. And with few exceptions, they've been overused and abused by the schools' office personnel until I wanted to rip the damn things out of the wall.

In fact, during my second year of teaching, I actually did climb up on my desk with a screwdriver and disconnect the wires. The principal of that particular school was obsessed with his PA system. For him, talking into that microphone was the pinnacle of school leadership. No one else was permitted to touch that PA system. "Did you notice the color of the leaves on the maple trees today, boys and girls?" he would croon into the microphone from his locked office, where no one could get to him. "I wish I had a necktie the color of those leaves."

My kids would groan, knowing they were in for at least five minutes of exhortations to keep off the grass and to avoid dropping candy wrappers, because they brought roaches. I disconnected the speaker because I thought these "announcements" robbed my class of instructional time, and encouraged students, with my tacit approval I suppose, to be rude to the disembodied voice coming from the brown box on the wall. We had a month's peace before my tinkering was discovered. Fortunately for my career I received only a mild reprimand from an assistant principal, who was no great fan of the broadcasts either.

One principal I worked for had a distinctive, if not unique style of starting our morning announcements. We'd hear a brief crackle of static. Then he would blow heavily into the microphone, twice. It always sounded as if a large bear was about to devour the entire PA console. But it *did* get our attention.

I can't understand the compulsion of many intercom announcers to say everything twice. "May I have your attention, please. May I have your attention, please. There will be a meeting of the newspaper club after school today in room 147. There will be a meeting of the newspaper club after school today in room 147." On top of that, the same announcements are repeated day after day. Aren't we trying to teach communications skills in school? When we repeat every instruction over and over, we're telling kids they don't have to bother to listen the first time. And they learn it fast.

Of course, timing is everything with school announcements. The announcement "Teachers--please hold your first period classes until ten o'clock this morning," is often made 30 seconds *after* we've dismissed our students to their second period teachers. We spend the next five minutes rounding up our wayward pupils and trying to settle them back down to work.

Then there are the endless interruptions. At one school I worked in, every class period was interrupted at least once or twice by school-wide bulletins: "Please excuse this interruption. Will Lamont Wilson report to the office." Repeated, of course. Don't they have Lamont's class schedule? In the three years that I worked at this school, no student of mine was ever called to the office. Not once. Nevertheless, every day my classroom activities came to a halt while someone in the main office tried to locate the elusive Lamont Wilson, whoever he is.

In this age of electronic miracles, surely school communications could be upgraded beyond primitive intercom technology. Electronics wizards have given us compact discs and fiber optics; scientists communicate around the world with microwaves and satellites. Surely they should be able to transmit a recognizable, understandable human voice between the school office and room 208. Why not install a telephone in each room? That way, when the office wants to tell us something, they can just ring us up. Or how about an unobtrusive computer terminal? I've visited one school where announcements silently scroll across a television monitor mounted in each room. Theoretically, I suppose a teacher could even turn the television off!

But one of the schools where I currently work may have the best system of all. It's an older building, constructed long before schools were wired for sound. There's no intercom at all! We get a daily bulletin in our mailbox each morning. If we want to find out what's going on, we read it. Announcements pertaining to students are read to them by a student at lunch each day. Once.

Unfortunately, the school has recently been invaded by electricians, who are hammering, drilling, and installing conduit and wiring. The school administration has decided to bring us into the electronic age. Finally after fifty years of peace and quiet, we're about to get an intercom in every room. I can hardly wait.

The Sandpaper, February 18, 1987

Incomprehensibly, in this digital age--with cell phones, wireless devices, wired classrooms, bluetooth, and student laptops and tablets--school administrators are <u>still</u> using the intercom to let teachers and students know what's going on, and to track down Lamont—with the same degree of success.

Scoring Our Schools

Standardized test scores for Virginia's local schools and school divisions have just been released. And once again we'll suffer from misunderstandings about what they mean. Surely there's a way to present test data so that the public gets honest and useful information from the results.

Each spring Virginia students spend about ten hours bubbling in answers to the Stanford achievement tests. These tests attempt to measure what kids have learned about reading, English, vocabulary, mathematics, science and social studies. The multiple choice tests are scored by computer. Months later, each student's results are reported as percentile scores.

This introduces the first area of confusion. A percentile is *not* a percentage. Let's say Jill Jones scores at the 55th percentile in reading. That does *not* mean that Jill got 54 percent of the questions right. Theoretically, it means that Jill scored better than 54 percent of all students who took the test. Jill may very well have answered 80 percent or more of the questions correctly. But that information never gets to her or her parents.

By the way, Jill's score is not *actually* compared with the other kids who took the test at the same time. It's compared with a small sample group that was used to "norm" the test, several years ago or more.

Jill's scores aren't reported in the paper, of course. What the public sees is a school-by-school and system-by-system average of these hundreds of individual performances. And this is where the whole process really goes wrong.

Standardized tests compare an individual child's performance with others of her age or grade. They are not designed to evaluate schools or school divisions. When a particular school's pupils average at the 50th percentile in reading, it does not mean that the school itself is achieving better than 49 percent of all schools. It is simply an average of individual student scores. As you would expect, many children will have scored above the 50th percentile, and others will have scored lower.

The truth is, a school's test averages say much more about the socioeconomic backgrounds of its students than they do about the quality of instruction the school provides. In addition, cultural biases built into the test may make it more difficult for minority student to score well.

You simply cannot tell how good a job a school is doing just by looking at average test scores. One school may serve students from families struggling for economic survival, with parents who have limited educations themselves. In such a school, teachers and staff may be doing an outstanding job and yet average test scores still might fall well below the 50th percentile. Meanwhile, another school serving highly privileged students could have test averages in the 65th percentile and yet be doing only a mediocre job of meeting student needs.

Unfortunately, the press and the politicians use test averages as a surrogate measure of educational quality. And too often school administrators defer to that view. Instead of pushing for educational excellence, they pressure teachers and building principals to raise test averages.

A principal I know works at a school with students from lower- and middle-income families. Their test averages are slightly below the 50th percentile. She says, "I've got a great faculty. Switch my entire staff to one of the schools in the affluent far West End. I guarantee we'd get those high test scores next year, and that other faculty would be just where we are--right around the middle."

The taxpaying public certainly has a right to know how our schools are doing. But our educational leaders must find a way to report test results, along with other data, so they more fairly represent what our schools actually accomplish.

Because each group of students is different, one alternative would be to compare the averages of a particular class with their own performance in prior years. For example, we should compare the eighth grade averages of the class of 2001 with their seventh grade and fourth grade averages. If the averages stay at about the same level over the years, then we know the school is doing a satisfactory job. If it goes up a few points, then we are exceeding expectations; if it goes down, we must identify where we need to improve.

Or, we could statistically combine the yearly changes in individual students' performances, to produce a measure of schoolwide or systemwide performance. Let's return to Jill's reading score. This year it was at the 55th percentile. Suppose that last year she scored at the 53rd. That's a net gain of two percentile points—an indication that she's continuing to achieve at about the same level, or perhaps slightly higher.

Now let's combine her net gain with the net gains or losses of all the other kids in her school. Suppose that averages out to about zero. Good! The students are holding their own, continuing their rate of achievement. If the average shows a gain of several points, even better! The school is doing something to increase student achievement. If there's a net loss of several points, we have to figure out what we can do to prevent students from slipping behind.

With test data now stored in computers, there's no reason to continue reporting this year's data unconnected to student performance from previous years.

And finally, we must remember that tests are only one measure of school success. Other considerations are important too. Are students safe, happy and enthusiastic? How many participate in the arts, music, sports or community service? What percentage graduate, or go on to higher education? Do students succeed in the workforce? Do they participate as citizens in our democracy? Do they keep learning as adults?

We ask an awful lot of our public schools. We should not be satisfied to measure what we get in return with a single questionable statistic based on students' performance on a multiple choice test.

Style Weekly, August 19, 1997

Shortly after this was written, Virginia schools stopped paying to measure student achievement with nationally-based norm-referenced tests like the Stanford Achievement test; instead, students are evaluated with the Standards of Learning test. Students and parents do get actual numbers of correct answers from each test now, along with information about the areas of knowledge in which they are weak or strong. That is, in some sense, an improvement.

On the other hand, SOL tests aren't normed to any group of students, so they don't offer any way to compare individual achievement with national averages. On several occasions, I analyzed the reading level of test passages while my eighth graders worked on their tests. I discovered that much of the material they had to read and respond to was written at the 10th or 11th grade level. That certainly seemed unfair. And too many of the questions still focus on specific, sometimes trivial facts rather than an understanding of important principles or thinking processes. How critical is it that Virginia students know the name of Robert E. Lee's horse?

The Educational Assembly Line
The SOLs are limiting our children's education.

What should we expect from our schools? Certainly we want children to read, write and compute. We want them to be able to think analytically and solve problems, to know basic information about our world, and become responsible citizens. They should learn to work together, and solve conflicts peacefully. We want them to develop an appreciation of the arts, and respect for cultures different from our own. We want children to learn skills that make them employable. We want to be sure they're healthy and well-fed, and want them to find life-long interests to make them happy.

How do we Virginians determine whether schools are meeting these expectations? We give kids a multiple choice test.

The Virginia Standards of Learning may be the most destructive thing politicians have done to public schools since "massive resistance." The problem is not so much the standards themselves--although they are written with far too much inflexible detail. (For example, one standard insists that students learn to use interactive video-discs, a technology that was obsolete five years ago.) It's the testing that makes the lives of Virginia educators and schoolchildren miserable, and robs them of a first-rate education.

This year, only 6.5 percent of Virginia's schools scored

high enough to meet accreditation standards. What does that tell us? When so many students fall short, one of the first things any good educator should ask himself is, "was there something wrong with the *test*?"

SOL testing has actually caused the curriculum to contract. Whatever doesn't fit within the standards gets eliminated. Educators in at least one local school district have already been told they will teach *nothing* other than SOL objectives until after next spring's testing window! Schools are forgoing field trips and cultural activities. Organizations like the Chesapeake Bay Foundation and local theater companies have experienced steep declines in the number of students they serve. Education, once a creative endeavor for many teachers and students, is becoming monotonous assembly-line labor.

Certainly we want schools to strive for excellence. But excellence cannot be judged solely on a single set of test scores. To assess students, staff, or entire schools this way is unfair, and contrary to everything we know about good educational practice. Not every child has the same interests, the same strengths, or the same level of ability. Some fifth graders may be ready to tackle seventh grade objectives; others are still struggling to master objectives from earlier years. Lockstep learning frustrates both groups.

Nor does every child do well under stressful test conditions. Fair assessment should also include teacher-made tests, daily classwork, and students' ability to apply what they've learned in discussions, writing and practical problem-solving.

Judging students and schools solely on test scores is particularly unfair when we consider economic and social factors. Look at which local schools scored best on last year's SOL tests. Now look at where they're located, and the socio-economic status of their students. The correlation couldn't be clearer. In most cases, schools serving affluent neighborhoods scored highest on the test. It's hard enough for kids to grow up poor in a land of plenty; a state test shouldn't penalize them further.

The SOLs are pushing some of the very best teachers to consider other careers. Wonderful, enthusiastic teachers believe they no longer have time for the projects that used to enliven their classrooms--the very activities that excite students about learning. Instead, they feel obligated to "teach the test," with uninspiring drills and frequent practice testing. More and more of their time is occupied with tedious recordkeeping.

In order to give students practice with "test-taking strategies," teachers are told to use more bubble-in multiple choice tests. By their very nature, multiple choice questions close off original thinking. Many of the questions on the actual SOL tests are well written and challenging. But even good multiple choice questions require less thought than other assessment methods such as essays, student-created products, or even questions answered with a student-generated word or sentence.

Is quality public education *really* at the top of our politicians' agendas? If so, why aren't private school students also required to take SOL tests? This exemption makes SOL testing look like a blueprint for sabotaging public education: Force public school kids take an overly-difficult set of tests. When they don't do so well, use the results to justify school vouchers or some other scheme to funnel public funds to private schools.

Fortunately there may be hope that decision-makers will be forced to reconsider the SOLs. An organization called Parents Across Virginia United to Reform SOLs is calling for major changes. These include an end to the use of SOL test results as a graduation requirement; the use of multiple criteria for student evaluation; and modification of the standards themselves to incorporate critical thinking and problem-solving skills, and to allow expansion and enrichment of the curriculum to meet community and individual needs. Parents' voices carry a lot of weight in public education; let's hope this effort continues to gather momentum.

Meanwhile, it seems school boards and superintendents either boast about good test results, or play the blame game and threaten employees over poor ones. Almost no one is questioning the validity of the testing itself. We need our educational leaders to advocate loftier goals for our public schools. I'd like to hear legislators, superintendents and school board members say, unequivocally, that they will not be satisfied to judge children, teachers or schools simply on the basis of a single battery of tests.

Style Weekly, Aug. 24, 1999

Unfortunately, PAVURSOL, the organization mentioned above, is long defunct, while the SOL testing program is still going strong.

Over the years, teachers and students managed to adapt to the SOLs—to the point where students in most schools were scoring well enough to achieve full accreditation. So, what did the state do? Raise the bar.

The test questions have become a "moving target." After several years in which most students scored well on the information they were expected to know, the state board of education decided to substantially increase the tests' level of difficulty. And to no one's surprise, student test scores crashed and all those schools who had been successfully educating their students are "failing" once again.

The Myth of Our "Failing" Schools

Everyone knows our nation's system of public education is in terrible shape. Schools are failing. Students are not getting the education they need and deserve. If we don't reverse this trend, and soon, U.S. children will continue to fall further and further behind in their ability to compete in our global economy. As Walter Williams wrote in a recent column, "There's no question that the American education system is in shambles. In our inner cities, education is nothing short of a criminal disgrace."

But sometimes, what everyone "knows" is wrong. Is public education really worse today than ever? I decided to see for myself. I wanted to look beyond anecdotal stories profiling a high schooler who graduated without learning to read, or students failing to make gains on standardized test scores. The bigger picture was readily available; all I did was look at education statistics in the most recent almanac.

I compared current high school and college graduation rates with rates from the recent past. If public education were failing, surely those percentages would be going down. But as it turns out, the "failure" of U.S. public education is a myth.

In 1960, only 41 percent of U.S. adults were high school graduates. Just forty years ago, almost 60 percent of U.S. adults had not completed high school! By 1998, the most recent year for which information was available, about 83 percent of Americans had finished high school. In the last forty years of the 20th century, the percentage of Americans with high school educations has *doubled*. Not surprisingly, at the same time, the high school dropout rate fell precipitously, from 27.2 percent in 1960 to 11.8 percent in 1998. For Black students, gains in high school completion were even more impressive, rising from only 20 percent in 1960 to 76 percent in 1998.

What about college graduation rates? Those figures are even more dramatic. In 1960, less than 8 percent of the public had four years of college; for African-Americans the figure was just over 3 percent. But by 1998, the percentages had quadrupled: for all Americans—24 percent; for African-Americans, 14.7 percent. Since 1950, when separate statistics were first available for Hispanic Americans, they too have made huge gains in both high school and college completion rates.

These statistics do not describe a system of public education in decline. In fact, this country has made huge and rapid advances in the effort to educate our entire population. And if we look a bit further back in history, there's even more evidence of how far we've come. Fifty years ago, most African American children attended inferior segregated schools. Look back just one hundred years ago, and you'd find an America in which most children in their teens weren't in school at all, because they'd already gone to work in the fields or factories.

The politicians and pundits who have convinced us that our schools are failing and in need of an emergency infusion of "higher standards" have sold us a bill of goods. It may be that "everyone knows" how bad our schools are, but the facts—which I found easily, in less than ten minutes—tell a different story.

So why are people like Walter Williams trying to convince us our schools are so awful? Perhaps it's simple ignorance. But his column may also provide a clue to his underlying agenda. After telling us how awful our public schools are, he proposes a solution: school vouchers and tuition tax credits. He claims only the "elite ignorance and arrogance" of politicians and bureaucrats keeps us from instituting such "reforms" to solve the problem.

At the risk of stating the obvious, this argument is simply backwards. It is the privileged "elite" of our society who would most benefit from tuition tax credits and vouchers. Public education belongs to *all* of us, whether or not our own children attend a public school. It's every taxpayer's investment in our nation's future. And for those who are economically disadvantaged, public education can unlock doors. Some students may choose not to walk through those doors, but they are open for everyone. And each time a student takes advantage of that opportunity, our entire society benefits.

I'm not claiming that public schools are perfect. Far from it. There's still much to be done before we can say we are helping each child reach his or her full potential. Public education is an imperfect human institution, as anyone who has been through the system knows. Some students still get passed along before they master the basic skills they need.

There are some great teachers, lots of okay teachers, and some terrible teachers. There are things of great value to be learned; and the impersonal, frustrating experiences typical of any large bureaucracy. There are bullies, social cliques, and inequities; and yet public school is still one of the greatest democratic institutions ever created.

Public schools, especially in our rural counties and inner cities, need more and better teachers, better facilities and equipment, and more exciting, inspiring curriculum. And they need the money that will allow them to afford those things. But despite all its shortcomings, public education is still one of the great American success stories. You could look it up.

Style Weekly, May 15, 2000

Reading Your Rights: The Tangled Web of Special Education Bureaucracy

The rights of every child to a Free Appropriate Public Education (otherwise known as FAPE) are protected by law. But for parents to find out just *how* those rights are protected, they'll have to wade through twenty-three pages of almost incomprehensible bureaucratic mumbo-jumbo.

If your child needs special education services, or is even "suspected to be in need" of such services, he or she has specific procedural safeguards. The U.S. Individuals with Disabilities Education Act guarantees it. This guaran-tee applies to a wide array of students: kids with severe physical or mental disabilities, kids with learning disabilities, kids with speech or hearing problems, and even kids who have been referred for study because a teacher thinks they are having difficulty and *may* need special services.

The safeguards give parents the right to see school records, to participate in educational planning for their child, and to receive notice of any proposed changes in their child's program. The procedures also place limits on a school administrator's ability to discipline these students for mis-behavior. Schools must hold a hearing to decide if a child's behavioral problems are a "manifestation" of his disability before disciplinary action can be taken. And, the safeguards provide parents with steps to follow—including appeals, hearings and civil court action--if they are dissatisfied with the school's decisions about their child's education.

All this is as it should be. Every child is entitled to an appropriate public education, and our government should ensure that right.

But here's where it gets strange. Parents *must* receive a copy of the "Procedural Safeguard Requirements" *each time* a child is referred for evaluation or reevaluation; when parents are notified of a meeting to develop or revisit an Individual Education Plan (IEP); when they request a due process hearing; and whenever they are notified of a disciplinary action. The document itself requires this. For some children, this might occur once or twice a year; for others notification may be required eight, ten or twelve times a year, or more.

Unfortunately, the document is twenty-three pages long, single spaced and written in complex, legalistic language certain to stymie the most literate of readers. Here's one sample sentence, from page 13:

"If, subsequently, a child with a disability who has a behavioral intervention plan and who has been removed from the child's current educational placement for more than 10 school days in a school year is subject to a removal that does not constitute a change of placement for disciplinary removals under 34 CFR § 300.519, the IEP team members shall review the behavioral intervention plan and its implementation to determine if modifications are necessary."

You couldn't make that stuff up if you tried. Imagine you're a parent sitting in the school office because your fourth grader has misbehaved. Maybe you had to take a couple of hours off from work. You're probably a bit irritated with both your child and the school. But before you hear about the problem, the principal or counselor hands you a twenty-three-page document. Most of it reads just like the paragraph above. "Please read this over and sign it," she says.

Now suppose you've struggled through to page 13 while you wait. How many times would you have to study that one sentence before you know whether or not the school is properly following procedures?

Many parents—parents who care about their children and want the best for them--simply won't be able to make sense of this document. Even *cum laude* college graduates will have trouble digesting twenty-three pages of such gobbledy-gook.

This process is nothing more than a bureaucratic game of "cover your butt." It allows school administrators to say, "Of course we informed the parents of their rights. See? There's their signature."

Surely there's a better way to protect the rights of special education students. Why hand parents a huge, indigestible, legalistic document? The basic rights described in those twenty-three pages could be summarized in a few simple statements on a single sheet of paper. Why not tell parents, "You have a right to see your child's school records," or "If you disagree with the school's decision, you can appeal?"

For parents who need further clarification or guidance in exercising their rights, schools can appoint and train ombudsmen from among their staff. They can have a copy of the full twenty-three pages available for anyone who wants to read them. They could even give each parent a set of the Procedural Safeguards once each year, on their first school visit.

Our schools currently expend untold reams of paper, along with copying expenses and staff time to follow the letter of the law, while its intent and spirit go unfulfilled. And knowing the educational bureaucracy, it's unlikely that we'll be doing something more sensible any time soon. So if a change in this process is to be made, parents will have to take the lead. Parents of special education students have fought a long battle to protect the educational rights of their children. Wouldn't it be great if those same parents demanded a short, clear, simple explanation of the rights they have worked so hard to establish?

Style Weekly, Sept. 1, 2004

Teaching Evolution

"Are you for it, or against it?"

It's the question I hear most often at signings for my new YA book about evolution. The first few times someone asked, I have to admit I was struck speechless. It was as if someone had asked if I were for or against weather, or the solar system.

Nevertheless, I think I grasp the misunderstandings that underlie the question. People in our country confuse *evolution* with the *theory of evolution*. And we misunderstand the meaning of the word *theory* itself.

Evolution is a fact of nature. Species gradually change over time. The evidence is extensive and indisputable. Scientists have observed species evolved within the span of our lifetimes. Bacteria, for example, have evolved resistance to antibiotics. Agricultural pests like potato bugs and boll weevils have evolved resistance to pesticides.

Beyond that, fossils provide thousands of examples of evolutionary pathways leading from earlier, extinct creatures to those currently inhabiting our planet. The fossil records of the evolution of whales and horses are particularly complete.

Most convincing is the evidence written in our own genes. All living things, from the simplest algae to the most complex arthropods and vertebrates, share the identical four-letter genetic code. Of course, each species' DNA is different.

The DNA in trout embryos tells them how to become trout, instead of dandelions, or manatees. But the coding itself is the same for all creatures. The three-base sequence G-A-T always means aspartic acid, one of the amino acids that are the building blocks of proteins. This is true whether the DNA comes from a trout, a dandelion, a manatee, or any other of Earth's organisms.

This shared genetic language means all living things almost surely share a common ancestor. Every creature now alive has descended from an unbroken line of organisms that succeeded in the struggle for survival. That line of inheritance can be traced back to the beginning of life itself. What an awe-inspiring idea. All life on earth is related. The evidence is right there, in our DNA.

Even before Charles Darwin published *The Origin of Species*, most scientists recognized that life evolves. What no one understood was the *cause* of evolution. Darwin's great idea—his *theory*—was not that species evolve, but that species evolve over vast expanses of time, little by little, through the process of natural selection.

No two individuals are exactly alike. Each bug or bullfrog varies in thousands of small ways from its brothers and sisters. Those slight variations provide the raw material for evolution.

Darwin realized most creatures don't survive to adulthood. Predators or environmental conditions kill off most individuals before they reproduce. But certain variations—perhaps a little extra speed or better eyesight or a more efficient digestive system—give some individuals a small advantage. Individuals with advantageous traits are more likely to survive long enough to reproduce. They then pass the advantages on to their offspring. In this way, over thousands of generations, nature gradually "selects" traits with survival value, and weeds out less successful characteristics.

In everyday speech, we use *theory* to mean an educated guess, as in "I have a theory about why I can't find a better job." In science, the term for such a supposition is *hypothesis*. For science, *theory* has a different, more specific and much broader meaning.

A scientific theory is a comprehensive explanation for a wide and seemingly diverse array of facts and observations. Darwin's theory gathered the many observations of evolution—fossil discoveries, the amazing diversity of life, slight variations among related species found on nearby island habitats, and many others. He then explained this speciation by describing the process of natural selection.

A successful theory must also predict results of observations yet to come. Darwin's theory has done that, repeatedly. Every year, paleontologists find more fossil ancestors of modern creatures, providing additional details about how life has evolved. Darwin himself, studying a Madagascar orchid with a nectar chamber sixteen inches deep, predicted that a pollinator insect must have evolved to take advantage of the flower's bounty. Fifty years later, scientists finally found it—a moth with a sixteen inch tongue!

So the success of a theory is not measured by "truth" or

falsehood, but rather its degree of success in accounting for observed phenomena. Theories are always subject to the test of new observations and experiments. There are always more questions to answer. Late in life, Darwin came to recognize that sexual selection also plays an important role in evolution—think peacock tails or moose antlers. Organisms choose mates based on appearance, behavior, success in combat, or other factors; these selections also influence the course of evolution. As science discovered the molecular mechanisms of heredity, unknown in Darwin's time, the theory of evolution was further modified and clarified. We now know evolution takes place at the genetic level, through modifications in DNA.

Darwin's theory of evolution through natural selection remains the bedrock of biological science. It allows biologists to look at any anatomical structure or behavior and ask "Why did that trait evolve? What advantage does it provide?" For our students to understand biology, Darwin's theory is as essential as Newton's laws are to the understanding of physics.

Currently a small group of media-savvy religious activists are trying to convince us that Darwin's theory is still controversial. Proponents of "intelligent design" argue that since modern evolutionary theory cannot answer every question about the origins of life, public school students should consider "other viewpoints." Some school boards and politicians have bought the argument. But there is no scientific evidence that contradicts the modern theory of evolution. There is *no* controversy about its acceptance within the halls of science.

True, biologists cannot outline every step in the evolution of life, and probably never will. There are still huge gaps in the fossil record. Many soft-bodied creatures didn't leave fossil evidence at all. And there are still facts that resist explanation, such as how feathered flight evolved, or why so many new life forms appeared at the beginning of the Cambrian period. There is still much to explore about the history of life.

And of course, there's the biggest question of all: How did life arise in the first place? It's a question that evolutionary theory does not and need not address. There's been much speculation and experimentation about the origins of life, of course. But no matter how life may have begun, evolution has proceeded ever since, through billions of generations, by natural selection. The fact that we don't know how life began in no way discredits evolutionary theory.

Life is extraordinarily complex and varied. It's hard to believe such complexity could arise through natural processes, without a designer's hand. But if a scientific concept is hard to believe, that doesn't make it wrong. A century ago, Einstein's realized that matter and energy are simply two different forms of the same thing—$E=mc^2$. That was hard to believe too, but it has since been proved true nonetheless, in explosively convincing fashion.

There is simply no verifiable scientific evidence that life was designed by some external, supernatural force. None. Intelligent design is not science, but a matter of faith. As with all matters of faith, people are free to believe as they choose. Darwin himself, as well as many other scientists, have maintained strong spiritual beliefs while simultaneously studying the world through scientific inquiry.

Faith can be taught freely in our nation, of course, but not in public schools. Public schools are secular institutions, supported by tax money raised from people of many different faiths—or none at all. That money cannot be spent to promote any one religious viewpoint.

Arguments for teaching intelligent design can be hard to resist. They are often couched in terms that promote diversity of thought, and scientific openness. But in the end, intelligent design is not science. The theory of evolution belongs in every public school biology classroom. Intelligent design belongs in the pulpit.

Style Weekly, Nov. 30, 2005

Maggie Walker's Diversity Complex
by Genevieve Siegel-Hawley and Paul Fleisher

The Maggie Walker Governor's School for Government and International Studies occupies the building of a formerly segregated city high school. Today the campus is home to one of the metropolitan area's premier educational institutions, drawing students from throughout the region. Ironically, the once all-black institution, named for a celebrated African-American female banker, serves a student population that is disproportionately white and overwhelmingly privileged.

During the past 10 years, Black students have applied to Maggie Walker at nearly four times the rate that they have been accepted. Blacks make up only 7 percent of Maggie Walker's student body even though they represent nearly 34 percent of the metro area's population and well over 20 percent of the school's applicants.

Recognizing these persistent inequities, two years ago the regional school board commissioned a study by four Curry School of Education faculty members at the University of Virginia. Their task was to identify and recommend best practices for the recruitment, identification and retention of underrepresented gifted minority students. The findings and recommendations from that report were presented in June. The Maggie Walker School Board and administration should move as quickly as possible to implement them.

The report outlines several easily-adopted recruitment strategies, such as offering a summer academic outreach program, recruiting potential students beginning at the fifth and sixth grade levels and adding information to the school web site emphasizing opportunities for diverse students. These recommendations certainly can be instituted during the upcoming school year.

In addition, many of the recommendations for identifying and selecting students could — and should — be implemented for the next round of applicants. Maggie Walker's current procedure uses multiple measures to evaluate students. Fifty of the possible 100 points are based on performance on several different ability and achievement tests; the remainder is earned through teacher recommendations, grades, a writing sample and a judgment about the degree of rigor in students' middle-school programs. The school then combines performance on each of these measures into a single numerical score.

Unfortunately, this averaging process renders the unique strengths and weaknesses of each student invisible to the admissions committee. And it often results in a situation in which students admitted to the school are separated by statistically insignificant decimal points from those placed on the waiting list or rejected.

The UVA study recommends that the admissions committee instead examine each student's measures separately, rather than as a single composite numerical score, basing admissions judgments on a review of a full profile of his or her achievement and potential. This would establish an admissions process similar to those used by selective colleges and universities.

The UVA report also identifies other concerns to be addressed once students from underrepresented groups are admitted to Maggie Walker. It advises the school to create a formal mentoring program for minority students, and a process for documenting students' reasons for withdrawal from Maggie Walker.

Based on our work with the school for a number of years, we suggest that the hiring of additional Black and Latino faculty members also should be a top priority for the School Board and administration, to generate greater community support and help the school attract and recruit a more diverse pool of student applicants.

A number of other recommendations from the report will likely require more detailed study prior to implementtation. For example, the admissions committee should begin collecting data to examine the reliability and validity of existing standardized tests, teacher recommendations and other data in predicting academic success at the governor's school. Maggie Walker should also consider — given its emphasis on government and international studies — whether Algebra I is an appropriate prerequisite or a roadblock to admitting otherwise-qualified students, as the study suggests.

The consistent underrepresentation of Black students at the school raises questions of both power and privilege. Maggie Walker Governor's School serves as a beacon of educational excellence, but for too long has sidestepped one of our most important principles: equality. The recent UVA report underscores the idea that excellence and equity are not mutually exclusive, and offers numerous strategies for promoting equal opportunities for our region's children. We encourage the Maggie Walker School Board and administration to begin fulfilling the school's stated mission to create "citizens who understand and celebrate diversity" by exploring and instituting such strategies immediately.

Style Weekly, August 12, 2009

Unfortunately, there's been very little change in the school's admissions process, and the inequitable results it continues to produce since Genevieve started working on this project. As of 2017, the school continues to use the same outmoded method of tallying all student data into a single numerical score—a procedure that hasn't been considered a best practice for more than 30 years. And Black and Latino students are still underrepresented in the student population.

It has been wonderful to watch Genevieve, one of my former middle school students, become a successful college professor, author and nationally recognized expert on school diversity. I've loved collaborating with her on this essay and the associated social justice project we've been working on for the past decade and a half. Dr. Genevieve Siegel-Hawley is one of many former students who have done well in fields including law, business, engineering, computer programming, performing arts and education. I can't imagine anything more gratifying.

Un-American

First grade. The first day of public school. The very first memory I can locate specifically in time and place. Our teacher leads us in a recitation of words I've never heard before. Yet somehow all the other students already have the words memorized, and join in. I'm surprised and puzzled. Why do all the other kids know this while I don't?

That afternoon I ask my mother why I don't know the Lord's Prayer like all the other kids. She explains to me that it's important in the Christian religion, but not in ours. It's not a prayer Jewish people say.

We are a tiny minority living in an overwhelmingly Christian community. So at age six, I'm faced with a dilemma. Should I learn this prayer and say it along with everyone else? That's up to you, my mother says. I could say it, or remain silent while everyone else recites, or she could even ask for me to be excused from the room during the prayer. That last choice isn't a consideration—I don't want to stand out from my classmates that much. Over the next few years I try both of the other options, but neither feels right. I want to be a full participant in my class, but I don't want to recite a prayer that's not part of my religious tradition. Eventually I settle on respectful silence.

The memory sticks with me to this day, more than half a century later. It was the first time, but by no means the last, that I would feel set apart from my classmates because of my religious heritage.

I can also remember the day the U. S. Supreme Court finally lifted this burden. In 1962, the court ruled that state-sponsored school prayer violated the constitutional separation of church and state. Public schools could no longer begin each day with an officially sanctioned prayer. My family felt both gratitude and relief that we no longer would have to sit through daily devotions outside of our own traditions.

Since then, I've had too many opportunities to wonder if and when that decision will be fully implemented. When I began teaching in Richmond in the mid-1970s, I was stunned to find some teachers starting each morning with Christian classroom devotions more than a decade after the Supreme Court's decision. I would walk down the hall and hear the Lord's Prayer echoing from several classrooms, even though some of our students were not Christian. Over the years, my own classroom has included Muslims, Jews, Buddhists, Hindus, Baha'is, and atheists, among others. If I wanted to lead my students in prayer, how could I choose?

And just a few weeks ago a Facebook friend posted a petition on *my* page calling for a return to prayer in public schools. I deleted it. A few days later, the same call was back again, posted by someone else. I deleted it once again.

Government-sponsored prayer even returned to the Virginia General Assembly this year. A constitutional amendment to allow school and government officials to lead organized prayer was introduced—despite the Supreme Court's ruling and the First Amendment's prohibition of any form of government-established religion.

Yes, some Americans still want to return institutional prayer to public school classrooms and other government functions, and even to take it upon themselves to select which prayers should be offered.

In fact, *nothing* in the Supreme Court's decision prevents individuals from praying in school or at government-sponsored events. Students and teachers are free to pray—privately--as often as they choose, to whomever they choose. Individuals attending government functions have that same right. But teachers, principals, school boards and other public officials may *not* make that choice for us. That's a core American principle. It's hard for me to understand why anyone in our nation would want it any other way.

So, let's be clear. In the United States, each of us is free to pray, or not, whenever and wherever we choose. However, no government official or school employee may lead public school children or a government meeting in government-organized and sponsored prayer. Our nation is composed of citizens from so many different backgrounds and beliefs that subjecting us to any one particular invocation will inevitably separate and divide us, rather than strengthening our moral and civic foundations.

Institutionalized prayer in public school or at other governmental functions is quite simply un-American.

Richmond Times-Dispatch, August 20, 2013

Politics—The Nuclear Arms Race and Other Campaigns

A Game Plan for Winning the Real Arms Race

I just realized I've been writing about the *wrong* arms race. The real nuclear arms race is the race between *us* and *the arms*. Unfortunately, the arms are way ahead at the moment, and the big question is whether humanity is going to catch up before we hit the finish line.

What we usually mean by the "nuclear arms race" is, of course, the competition between the United States and the Soviet Union to build new and more efficiently destructive nuclear warheads and "delivery systems." But that race is long over. Both of our nations crossed that finish line years ago.

The Soviet Union and the United States were in a genuine race during the 1940s, '50s, and early '60s. Who would be the first to develop a thermonuclear weapon? Who could build the first intercontinental bomber, the first intercontinental missile? Who could make their warheads smaller and more easily deliverable? The United States won most of those heats, but it turned out not to matter very much, because the Soviets weren't far behind. Now, twenty years later, it matters not at all that the United States outran the Soviets by a few years in our ability to annihilate an enemy anywhere on the globe.

The race to build our countries' nuclear arsenals was effectively over by the late 1960's. By then each of us had the undisputed ability to destroy the other's society, even after our own nation had been devastated. The new global strategy that our military planners created to match this state of affairs became known as "mutually assured destruction," or MAD. In theory, the knowledge that we will completely destroy one another in a nuclear "exchange" prevents each of us from using our nuclear weapons.

The strategy seems to have worked, so far. But if we rely on it forever, sooner or later some accident or miscalculation will destroy us. Human beings do make mistakes, after all.

Unfortunately, our governments have failed to recognize that the nuclear arms race is over; we've continued full speed ahead. The continued racing has been enormously profitable for U.S. military contractors and their stockholders. Companies like General Electric, Morton Thiokol, DuPont and AT&T have made billions of dollars from the endless cycle of nuclear escalation. And many a politician has been elected by playing on public fears that the United States is "falling behind" the Russians.

But the continuing escalation hasn't done the rest of us any good at all. We certainly aren't safer than we were twenty years ago. And our pockets are much emptier. We've built a huge national debt, dumping billions of dollars into weapons development.

Meanwhile, research into civilian technology, which

could generate long-lasting economic wealth and improve the world's standard of living, has been starved for funding.

If all we really want is a believable deterrent, a few hundred warheads based on virtually invulnerable nuclear submarines would be sufficient. We could easily junk 95% of our warheads and still retain the ability to lay the entire Soviet Union to waste, with plenty of weapons left over.

Instead, we now possess 30,000 nuclear warheads, deployed in underground silos, in submarine missile tubes, on Pershing and cruise missiles in Europe, on long and medium range bombers, even in artillery shells, torpedoes and land mines.

What do those extra thousands of warheads get us? Increased danger of accidental nuclear war or nuclear terrorism, growing stores of deadly plutonium, vastly expensive weapons research and the continuing billions for production, maintenance and deployment of nuclear armaments. They earn us the distrust of the world's non-nuclear nations and subtly color each day of our lives with dread and uncertainty.

So, what must we do to win the *real* arms race? First of all, we can't afford to drop out of the race in despair, just because we're far behind. The stakes are too high. Giving up will only guarantee that eventually we'll all lose. Instead we have to get into training. This race isn't going to be won with a sprinter's quick burst of speed; we're in a marathon. Reducing and eventually eliminating nuclear weapons will take a long time and lots of effort.

Reverting to a peacetime economy and a peacetime attitude will be difficult. Many powerful elements of our society now have a vested interest in building weapons and maintaining a warlike posture. Workers in every Congressional district earn their livings from the arms race. Their jobs must be converted to civilian production.

The cold war vision of a divided, antagonistic world has become deeply engrained in our national consciousness. We must replace this view with a new, realistic vision of our nation as one member, albeit a wealthy and powerful one, of a cooperative community of nations. These changes will require an investment of years of effort.

Winning the real arms race will also take teamwork. Nuclear weapons hinder the efforts of every group working for equality, social justice and a better life for people everywhere in the world. The arms race robs the poor of food, housing and medical care. It confounds our efforts to solve the problems of drug abuse, education, race and gender discrimination. It undermines our businesses by adding to huge national deficits and cripples civilian scientific research and technological growth.

Virtually every "special interest group" has an interest in nuclear disarmament. To win our race, we'll all have to work together, using all the resources at our disposal, from computer chats to simple neighbor-to-neighbor conversations, from vigils and demonstrations to lobbying and electoral politics.

Ten years ago, few people even mentioned nuclear

weapons in public discussions. Five years ago, the nuclear freeze movement was just beginning to capture our attention. Today, nuclear policy is discussed on the nightly news, a majority of the U.S. Congress favors a comprehensive nuclear test ban, and even President Reagan has felt the winds of change and become a born-again advocate of arms control.

We're still far behind in our race against the nuclear menace, but it looks like we've started to make up some lost ground. Let's hope so. We're running the race of our lives.

The Sandpaper, August 12, 1987

Since the 1980s, the U. S. has substantially reduced the number of nuclear weapons we deploy around the world—as has Russia. But there are still thousands of nuclear warheads and their delivery systems ready for launch at a moment's notice—or a momentary mistake. We still have a <u>long</u> way to go.

Living In Glass Houses

During the past year we've paid a great deal of attention to the disgraceful system of racial segregation in South Africa. Only a very few years ago America had its own Apartheid laws. But our national consciousness has changed. We've come to recognize and deplore South African Apartheid as a brutal, repressive system that keeps the black majority in South Africa in political and economic bondage to the privileged white minority.

Yet South Africa is a relatively easy target. It takes little effort or sacrifice to point our fingers across the sea in condemnation. Racial segregation and exploitation in America is a much harder problem to address successfully. To face Apartheid squarely, Americans must use South Africa as a mirror to see how much farther we ourselves have to go in healing our own society. There is still devastating racial inequality here in our own nation, our own city. If we really believe Apartheid is evil, let's end it here.

There is Apartheid in Richmond housing. Yes, some neighborhoods are integrated and laws prohibit discrimination in housing. But in fact, most Richmond neighborhoods are segregated. Many real estate agents conspire to keep it that way, by "steering" white clients to white neighborhoods and Black clients to Black neighborhoods. You don't have to be a building inspector to see that Black neighborhoods have more than their share of substandard housing. Landlords seem less concerned about inadequate, dangerous heating equipment, infestations of rats and cockroaches, flaking paint, and broken plumbing when these problems occur in Black neighborhoods. Our city's leaders may speak with pride of its downtown renaissance, but they need only drive a few blocks from the glittering new shops and offices to see how incomplete that rebirth still is.

There is Apartheid in Richmond's schools. Despite the fact that the public school system has capable teachers and spends a great deal of money to educate its students, many of its schools are almost totally segregated. A large number of the students attending these schools come from poor families; some are undernourished and inadequately clothed.

We have a two-tiered educational system. The public schools serve an inordinate percentage of economically disadvantaged children and children with special needs, while private schools cater to privileged, mostly white students. Such a system is inherently unequal and our city will pay the price of that inequality for years to come.

There is Apartheid throughout our economy. Black Americans average less than 60% of the income of white Americans. Unemployment is about three times higher for Black workers than white workers; for young Black men, the figure is even worse.

Our city has too few Black doctors, stockbrokers, architects and systems analysts. Black workers hold an inordinate percentage of the lower paying, less skilled jobs in our city. These jobs provide honorable work, but they don't pay well and provide little prestige. Businesses in Black neighborhoods often don't provide the same quality or selection of merchandise that can be found in white neighborhoods. But their prices are just as high, or even higher than those in the suburban malls. And inner city residents without cars have no public transportation to allow them access to those suburban malls and office parks for shopping or employment opportunities.

There is Apartheid in public health and safety. Black Americans have a shorter life expectancy than whites, and Black infant mortality rates in some U.S. cities exceed that of some third world countries. Here in Richmond, as elsewhere, Black citizens are victims of crime far more often than whites.

Although many of Richmond's top political posts are now held by Black leaders, racial inequality and segregation is still deeply rooted in our city. The causes of this problem are as old as our history of slavery, repression and exploitation. We can't change our history, but much can be done to correct for its effects.

For example, aggressive affirmative action programs, tax incentives for minority hiring and training programs, and low-interest loans for minority-owned businesses would move us toward economic equality. So would scholarships and loans for promising Black students who want to hone their skills in college and then bring them back to benefit our city.

Attendance zones drawn to include children of diverse

socio-economic backgrounds, extra programs designed to make public schools more attractive places for *all* students, and commitments from more white parents to educate their children in the schools their taxes support would help rid our school system of segregation. Aggressive enforcement of housing codes and neighborhood revitalization programs would help ameliorate inequities in housing.

In no way am I suggesting we abandon opposition to Apartheid in South Africa. We certainly should focus whatever pressure we can on the South African government. If disinvestment will add to that pressure, then by all means let's disinvest. If boycotts of companies that do business with South Africa add to that pressure, then let's boycott. If cutting off exports of advanced technology will help, let's do that too. People fighting for freedom in South Africa must know that Americans support their struggle with deeds as well as words.

But South Africa is far away. Actions such as those are really the easiest part of our task. They may give us a warm feeling of having done the right thing, but they involve minimal cost to our own lives.

If we want to see an end to Apartheid, the strongest action we can take is to end it here. Then our attempts to influence the policies of other nations will have a moral authority that can be purchased no other way. We'll *know* a nation can thrive without racial inequality, because we'll have done it ourselves.

Style Weekly, May 27, 1986

It's Time to Stop Bombing Nevada

Since August 1985, there have been over 20 nuclear explosions in the Nevada desert. During that time, the Soviet Union has exploded no nuclear weapons. But unless President Reagan or the United States Congress takes action, February 1987 will mark the end of the Soviet moratorium on nuclear testing.

General Secretary Gorbachev announced a halt to Soviet testing on August 6, 1985—the 40th anniversary of the bombing of Hiroshima. He invited the United States to join his nation in a temporary halt of all nuclear tests, while a permanent, comprehensive test ban treaty is negotiated.

The moratorium was originally scheduled to last through 1985. But the Soviets have extended it three times since then, most recently until the end of 1986. Meanwhile, the Reagan administration has consistently refused to join in. Instead, the U.S. has continued to test.

Now, after seventeen months, the Soviets say they cannot extend their unilateral moratorium further. They will resume testing after the first U.S. nuclear test of 1987, unless new negotiations towards a test ban treaty begin. That first U.S. test is scheduled to take place in early February. And so a precious opportunity to bring at least a part of the nuclear arms race under control may slip away.

It's unfortunate President Reagan hasn't taken the

Soviets up on their offer. Reaching a test ban agreement with the Russians would be easy, and popular. According to a recent Gallup poll, Americans favor a comprehensive test ban by a margin of almost two to one. Both houses of the U.S. Congress have passed resolutions in support of a test ban by overwhelming margins.

And this summer the House passed a bill eliminating all funds for nuclear testing for as long as the Soviets continued their moratorium. This provision was later traded away in conference with the Senate, just prior to the confused, failed talks in Reykjavik.

The United States is formally committed to negotiating a comprehensive test ban. The Threshold Test Ban Treaty of 1974 requires both the U.S. and Soviet Union to continue test ban talks. Negotiations were almost completed in 1980, under the Carter administration. But President Reagan abandoned the talks shortly after taking office. Nevertheless, the framework of the treaty still exists. Only minor details remain to be worked out.

We don't even need to "trust" the Russians in order to reach a testing agreement with them. We have the technical means to know if they cheat. You can't hide a nuclear explosion, even underground. Satellites and seismic monitoring stations can detect nuclear tests. Recently the Soviets also agreed to on-site inspections, long an obstacle to reaching a treaty agreement. They have already permitted a private group of U.S. scientists to set up and maintain one monitoring site on Soviet soil.

A test ban would do our nation and the rest of humankind a world of good. Now that the U.S. has discarded the SALT II agreements, we need more than ever to find some common ground with the Soviets. Just knowing the superpowers could agree on one arms control matter would make billions of people all feel a bit more confident about their own futures. Reaching such an agreement could reverse the momentum of the arms race, and establish a cooperative atmosphere that could make additional arms agreements easier to achieve.

A test ban would also slow the development of new weapons that U.S. and Soviet designers may be dreaming up. Existing nuclear weapons designs are almost never tested for reliability by exploding them in the desert--they are tested component by component using non-nuclear procedures. It's the new designs that are exploded in Nevada.

A test ban wouldn't weaken our nuclear deterrence. We already have enough warheads to destroy one another ten or fifteen times over. The world's nuclear arsenals have an explosive power equivalent to more than 7,000 time *all* the ordnance exploded during World War II—including the two bombs dropped on Hiroshima and Nagasaki. If that's not sufficient deterrence against an enemy attack, then nothing will be.

One new weapon that would be stalled by a test ban is the nuclear-pumped laser. That's the part of President Reagan's Star Wars defense that promises to surround the planet with hundreds of orbiting H-bombs. Theoretically, in the microsecond they explode, these weapons would shoot down enemy missiles with laser beams. Proponents of this technology have said very little about what happens in the ensuing microseconds, as several hundred H-bombs explode in massive fireballs above our atmosphere. This ill-conceived idea should remain undeveloped and untested forever.

Then there's the issue of nuclear proliferation. No one wants another dozen or so countries to build their own nuclear weapons. But if the superpowers can't slow the growth of their own arsenals, what incentive is there for Argentina, Pakistan, Israel or South Africa to restrain their nuclear research and development? In fact, the U.S.-ratified Nuclear Non-Proliferation Treaty *requires* us to take further steps toward disarmament.

Finally, there are other, more mundane considerations. U.S. Nuclear testing costs almost a billion dollars each year. We already know the warheads work, all too well. Why not save some money? We could reduce the deficit, build new housing, or feed needy citizens. And we'd also be doing some good for the environment. Years of nuclear tests have ravaged the Nevada desert, and sent occasional plumes of radiation hundreds of miles downwind. A test ban would let that fragile environment begin to heal.

This year peace activists in Richmond and around the nation will continue to focus their efforts on the need for a comprehensive nuclear test ban. In fact, these men and women represent a far larger group of citizens who are tired of endless escalations of the arms race, endless requests for military spending, and endless anxiety about the deadly threat hanging over our heads.

Public pressure against atmospheric nuclear testing in the '50s and early '60s played the major role in bringing about the Limited Test Ban Treaty of 1963. People around the world knew that radioactive fallout was endangering their children. After only six weeks of negotiations, all nuclear tests in the atmosphere, in the ocean and in space were outlawed.

Now it's time to complete the process. It's time to stop bombing Nevada. Those of us who are quietly fed up with seeing our tax dollars being vaporized in the Nevada desert must make those feelings known. And Congress needs to show the President it means business too, by passing a bill that cuts off funds for nuclear testing for as long as the Soviets continue their halt. After that happens, it shouldn't be much longer before the Senate is ratifying a comprehensive test ban treaty.

Style Weekly, January 27, 1987

Still waiting . . .

Binary Weapons: Reagan 1, Sanity 0

On July 29, 1986, the Reagan administration announced it was giving the go-ahead for production of a new generation of chemical weapons. It's been about twenty years since the United States made its last nerve gas bomb. In fact, the Army is now destroying its aging stockpiles of nerve gas bombs and shells—very carefully, we hope. But with the conditional approval of Congress, the military is about to have its arsenals restocked with a new generation of binary nerve gas.

This new type of weapon is composed of two "harmless" chemicals that combine to form a deadly gas that paralyzes the nervous system and kills in seconds. Theoretically, the two chemicals are to be combined only when such a weapon is about to be used.

What eludes me in the discussions of this new system of indiscriminate mass destruction is any reasonable explanation of why we need it at all. The Reagan administration claims it favors a verifiable ban on all chemical weapons. But in the meantime, they say we need chemical weapons to deter the Soviet Union from using its chemical weapons. Does this make any sense?

For years, the Reagan administration has been castigating the Soviets for using or supplying chemical weapons in Afghanistan and Southeast Asia. Never mind that many scientists believe the infamous "yellow rain" was nothing more than bee droppings. Let's suppose that the Soviets have in fact been guilty of using chemical weapons. How should our nation respond? Does it make more sense to join the rest of the world as we express outrage, or join the Soviets in the same detestable efforts we accuse them of perpetrating?

The first alternative gives us the moral high ground, and places us firmly on the side of a hundred smaller nations who may feel threatened by Soviet and U.S. military might. Yet inexplicably, the Reagan administration has chosen to get down in the gutter with its Soviet adversaries, giving the rest of the world one more reason to despise us both in equal measure.

How does the administration justify stockpiling new supplies of nerve gas? Deterrence. They claim that by producing our own supplies of chemical weapons, we deter the Soviet Union from attacking our forces in Europe with theirs. It's hard to believe anyone deliberated for even one moment before presenting this rationalization for this latest escalation of the arms race.

For a deterrent to be effective, there must be a commitment to actually use it if the attack it is supposed to prevent ever happens. For U.S. nerve gas to be a believable deterrent, our nation must be willing to use it in battle. And the rest of the world must be made to believe that we will do exactly that.

So the Reagan administration's decision to produce nerve gas tells the world our country will use such weapons on the battlefield. Undoubtedly, the rest of the world finds this stance despicable. Do we *really* want to release nerve gas over

Europe or some other part of the world, and earn ourselves a place in history—whatever history may be left—alongside the butchers of the Nazi holocaust? I trust the majority of U.S. citizens are unwilling to take such an action.

But the deterrence argument is bankrupt for another, even larger reason. With its nuclear arsenals, the United States already has far more deterrent power than it could ever need. We have enough nuclear warheads to destroy the Soviet Union ten times over. Our government's policy has been unequivocal about where it draws the line. If the Soviets overrun Western Europe, we will use our nuclear weapons. Advocates of a "peace through strength" philosophy claim this policy of deterrence has kept Europe free from war for forty years.

So what's the nerve gas for? If our nuclear weapons are an effective deterrent against Soviet aggression, why do we need binary chemical weapons? If the threat of total annihilation in a nuclear holocaust doesn't deter a Soviet attack, then surely a supply of deadly chemicals won't make the least bit of difference.

No matter how you look at it, the production of new chemical weapons is a losing proposition for our country. It doesn't make us safer, and it damages our image in the eyes of the world.

Let's assume that the Soviet Union is still in the business of producing chemical weapons. How should we deal with that threat?

Let's use a simple bit of international *jujitsu*: the

Soviets are sensitive to world opinion. Their year-long moratorium on nuclear testing shows how far they will go to display peaceful intentions to the rest of the world. The United States can take advantage of this by refusing to participate in a chemical arms race, thereby focusing the pressure of international disapproval on the Soviets. Since a chemical arsenal provides no additional deterrence anyway, our country has nothing to lose by such a stand, and a great deal of international good will to gain.

The Reagan administration is so caught up pursuing the chimera of military superiority that it can't see how poor a choice it has made. Perhaps the U.S. Congress will exercise a wiser, more realistic vision, and prevent our country from wasting any more of our resources on this particular military horror.

The Sandpaper, August 13, 1986

The Children Need to Know: Teaching about Nuclear War

Children need and want to know about nuclear war. Nuclear weapons are one of the most awesome, dreadful aspects of their world, often mentioned in newscasts, but rarely discussed by the adults in their daily lives. Listen to these comments from some of my seventh-grade students as they discussed the nuclear arms race:

"You could say I have a personal interest in preventing nuclear war."

"I want to know more about how the bombs actually work."

"I don't like thinking about it, but I know it's very important."

These students had been studying *Choices,* the junior high school unit on conflict and nuclear war produced by the Union of Concerned Scientists and the National Education Association in 1983. *Choices* and other materials that teach about this difficult and terrible subject have created much controversy in the past several years. But it seems strange and frightening that teaching about nuclear issues should create any dissension at all.

There is no responsible segment of our society, from the most conservative to the most liberal, in favor of an uncontrolled arms race. Ronald Reagan may not favor a nuclear freeze, but he has consistently supported some form of arms control, in words if not in deeds. In a speech to the U N on September 26, 1983, the President said, "...we wish to negotiate arms reductions, and to achieve significant, verifiable arms control agreements."

In his second term, arms control has become a centerpiece of his foreign policy. Republican Senator and former Navy Secretary John Warner of Virginia says, "We are indebted to the growing number of Americans...speaking out urging the leadership of all nations to...eliminate--as near as humanly possible--the risk of even a single nuclear detonation as an accident or act of aggression." *Parade* magazine, the Sunday supplement to 30 million American newspaper readers, could hardly be closer to the center of American political thought. It encouraged its readers to write the presidents of the United States and the Soviet Union urging control of the arms race.

With the continuing public concern about nuclear weapons, we might expect the subject would also make appropriate material for the social studies or science classroom. It's hard to imagine how a teacher of U.S. history, civics, or physical science could justify avoiding discussions of nuclear weapons. But resistance to including the study of this issue in school curricula has been widespread, both within and outside the educational system.

Check the textbooks and curriculum guides used in your local school system. If they are anything like the ones in my district, they are virtually silent on the topic of nuclear weapons. Our middle school American history textbooks do mention that the United States dropped two atomic bombs on Japan to end World War II. They also tell students that the Limited Test Ban Treaty and Strategic Arms Limitation Treaty have since banned "several types of weapons."

That's it. One and a half paragraphs in 350 pages of American history. Is that how responsible educators should deal with the most pervasive political and military fact of the past forty years? Clearly, teachers and parents need to make use of supplementary reading material and resources like *Choices* to fill out our children's education, at least until more complete information is incorporated into their texts.

Perhaps the main reason that the nuclear issue has been given so little attention in our curricula and our classrooms is that it is so enormously terrifying. Psychologists call it "denial." How can we live anything resembling a normal life knowing that this terrible threat hangs over our heads every minute of every day? We don't want to think about the prospects of blinding multi-megaton blasts, deadly fallout, and the social and ecological devastation that would follow the detonation of even a small fraction of the world's stockpiles of nuclear weapons. So we push the subject from our minds, and neglect it in our classrooms and family discussions.

But in so doing, we deny our children the opportunity to consider a topic of paramount importance, and we set a poor example of responsible adulthood. Our republic works best when an informed public considers the issues of the day from all viewpoints. Citizens must examine our country's policies and make informed choices. As parents and educators our task is to give children the skills and knowledge they need to become effective adults and citizens. Sometimes that means discussing subjects that are uncomfortable or frightening.

Children watch the evening news, too. Many junior high and even elementary-age children are aware of nuclear weapons. Several years ago, about half of my seventh graders said they had thought about nuclear weapons and knew some basic information about the arms race. In the past several years, thanks to wider news coverage of nuclear issues, television specials, and magazine features, more and more students seem to be informed, interested, curious or concerned.

Surely most teachers hear unsolicited comments or questions about nuclear weapons from their students, and find expressions of concern in their writings. Yet we have no curriculum materials to help our students face their fears or conquer their ignorance. And too many of us need to take those same steps ourselves.

When children talk about nuclear weapons, they are often intensely interested in getting factual information. At times, feelings of confusion and helplessness seem to dominate. Their actual knowledge of the subject is often very limited. Most don't understand the theory of deterrence, or the physics of how nuclear weapons work, or the history of their development and deployment. When I ask which country, if any, has ever used the bomb in warfare, most don't know. Not surprisingly, given the current state of international relations, many guess it was the Soviet Union. That one paragraph in their social studies book obviously hasn't made much of an impression.

Children don't understand how Americans got into the situation in which we now find ourselves. They may have heard of "radiation," "fallout," or "megatons" but most don't understand what those terms mean. They've probably never heard of the Limited Test-Ban Treaty or SALT, two of the most hopeful events in the history of the arms race. Many aren't familiar with the arms control efforts our government is currently engaged in, or those which citizens groups are proposing. In short, they know there's something dangerous and threatening in their world, but generally haven't mastered the most basic information about that terrible threat.

I often wonder how many of the other problems our students face are tied to the underlying menace of nuclear war. Children make important life choices with the fact of a runaway arms race lurking in the background. Consciously or unconsciously they know their futures can be wiped out at any moment by the flick of a switch or the failure of a computer chip.

Should we be surprised if some students seem apathetic or have difficulty working towards long-range goals? When they fall into the escapism of promiscuity, drugs or alcohol? Should we be surprised that many don't have enough faith in their own future to strive for excellence in their scholastic endeavors? I strongly suspect that a safer, more stable world would help promote healthier, more responsible and more stable students.

Our job as educators includes informing our students, encouraging them to become active, involved citizens, and safeguarding their physical and emotional welfare. Surely this should include teaching them about nuclear weapons. Our students need to know, because their limited awareness unsupported by basic factual information is terrifying. Instead of nameless fears, our children need to begin experiencing a sense of their own power as citizens, as they join with the adults around them to face this difficult dilemma.

We can teach children the history of the past forty years, including the history of the arms race. We can explain the physics of fission and fusion. We can include nuclear issues when we talk about current events. We can even let them know about our personal concerns and commitment to ending the arms race, so they know they are not alone in their fears. If we don't, we're shirking our responsibilities as adults, and evading the most critical issue of our time.

Phi Delta Kappan, November, *1985 (One side of a "Point/Counterpoint" discussion about the* <u>Choices</u> *curriculum)*

Babes in Arms

Skyfire assault helicopter
81 mm mortar
Night Raven S3P Jet fighter
Mauler manned battle tank
M-60 high-powered machine gun
Uzi sub-machine pistol
M-33 grenade
MX-7 -- The Ultimate Weapon

The Pentagon's wish-list for the upcoming year's budget? A procurement order for the Rapid Deployment Force? No, parents of young children may recognize this catalog of mayhem as a part of Santa's shopping list.

You can find all these weapons in the "guns and action figures" section of your favorite toy store, along with dozens of others ranging from laser guns to grenades and rocket launchers. In case you're wondering, the Uzi is recommended for ages three and up. To use the ultimate weapon, your child should be at least five.

This is the season when much of the world celebrates the birth of the Prince of Peace. But if you visit a toy store during this season, one of the things you will see is an extensive array of weapons being sold as gifts for children. The amount of shelf space devoted to playtime death and destruction seems to have increased significantly in recent years. Toy stores carry just about anything the well-equipped toddler might need to settle a border dispute or fight off roving bands of terrorists.

In addition to old standards such as swords, daggers, pistols and rifles, you can also arm your offspring with sawed-off shotguns, machine guns, anti-tank guns, tanks and bombs. There are also helmets, belts and even tiny camouflage suits. I was unable to locate a nuclear warhead, but I'm sure some enterprising toymaker will have one on the market before too long.

Much of this equipment is spun off from military action movies and TV shows, and marketed under the names of various celebrities or fictional characters. You can get the Chuck Norris Karate Kommado Weapons Pack, the Schwarzenegger Commando M-33 Grenade, and dozens of items featuring the greased, grimacing image of Sylvester Stallone as Rambo.

The Rambo line also features its own "ultimate weapon," the LZ-10. The young store clerk couldn't tell me what might happen when this ultimate weapon goes up against the aforementioned MX-7.

There is also a massive amount of ordnance for the G.I. Joe "action figure." The packaging refers to G.I. Joe as "A Real American Hero," and pictures him blazing away at unseen enemies with whatever weapon happens to be in the box. If this four-inch piece of plastic is an American hero, *real* America is in a lot of trouble.

Is this massive buildup of war toys, and their associated TV shows and movies a portent of the future facing our nation? These toys offer a dangerous vision of an isolated America facing a hostile world. They glorify muscular, white males armed to the teeth with the latest technology "defending freedom" by doing battle with unidentified enemy "terrorists." Our children are not going to be able to address the economic and political complexities of the modern world if that one-dimensional viewpoint hardens into their adult view of our planet.

One line of war toys is called the "MX-12 Defender Force--Defenders of Freedom." The irony is inescapable. I don't suppose there would be much of a market for a Mahatma Gandhi "action figure." But when they hear "defenders of freedom," I wish America's children would learn to think of Thomas Jefferson, Jane Addams or Martin Luther King, Jr. Instead they may be learning that freedom can only be defended at the point of a gun.

I have a friend, a mother, who's worried about all this. Her sweet five-year-old son sees these exciting gadgets advertised on television. His playmates bring them to school. He wants an assault rifle of his very own too.

But my friend is looking a little farther ahead. She's thinking about the day her young son will turn eighteen. Draft age. She wonders if our toy manufacturers are helping to teach a new generation to accept and love the implements of war, so that when they grow up, they'll willingly march off to die in Nicaragua or the Middle East or some other "trouble spot" where things aren't going just the way our government would like them to. She believes playing with toy weapons in childhood makes it too easy to accept massive buildups of real weapons later, in our all-too-real adult world.

My friend is in a quandary. The pleading requests of a five-year-old can be hard to resist. She doesn't want to restrict her son's experiences. But she also doesn't want him to learn to love the toys of war.

So what does she do? She's managed to come to her own personal arms-control agreement. First of all, she won't buy her son any guns, tanks, or bombs. She simply refuses to spend her money on weapons, even if they are only toys. She gladly spends her money to satisfy his other wants instead. Second, she explains this decision to him when he asks for a war toy, as he does more often than she would like.

And third, because she doesn't want him to see these toys as "forbidden fruit", she does allow her son to play with his friends' tanks, bombs and G.I. Joes, although this does require her to smile at him through clenched teeth at times.

It seems like a sensible solution to a difficult dilemma, although the real test won't come for a few years when the boy becomes a young man. If enough mothers and fathers were to reach similar accommodations with their young sons, perhaps we'd never have to watch another generation march unquestioningly off to war.

Peace on earth, goodwill toward men. It's a beautiful, holy idea. But like my friend, each of us will have to *do* something if we want to make it a reality. Resisting the escalating arms trade for children seems like one small step in the right direction.

Style Weekly, December 2, 1986

Note: I'm happy to report that since this was originally written, my friend's child has grown into a fine young man, a successful high school teacher and coach, and a father himself.

Meanwhile, far too many young children are injured or killed playing with real firearms they find unsecured in their home, or their friends' homes. And let's not forget 12-year-old Tamir Rice, killed by Cleveland police while playing with a toy replica gun.

Meanwhile, the children I wrote about in the 1980s are now young adults—and too many of them are walking around town toting semi-automatic rifles or wearing sidearms on their hips, in a display of support of open-carry laws and the Second Amendment. Hmm....

Keep Your Fingers Crossed, Virginia

When I voted against the proposed Virginia lottery last year, I didn't cast my ballot out of a sense of righteous disapproval. I don't think gambling is necessarily sinful. I'm sure a friendly poker game or an afternoon at the track offers plenty of entertainment value. I voted against the lottery mainly because I saw it as a hidden, regressive tax, raising millions of dollars of revenue from those who can least afford to pay. And I voted against it because I didn't want the state raising money by raising false hopes--encouraging people to go for the big score instead of trying to improve their lot through their own efforts.

Nevertheless, I didn't feel strongly enough to go out and campaign against the idea. If the voters of Virginia decided they wanted a lottery--and they clearly did--I figured they should get the chance to give it a try.

Well, we've had our first trial. Match Three, the first lottery game, earned the distinction of being the second most successful state lottery kickoff ever. Only Florida's lottery got off to a faster start. The state is raking in money at almost twice the anticipated rate; Virginians bought one hundred million lottery tickets, at a dollar a piece, in about a month's time.

Match Three brought about $35 million into the state's general fund. Lottery retailers are pulling in the money too--about $5 million for the first game. And so far, nothing I've seen has convinced me that I pulled the wrong lever last November. In fact, the more I see of the Virginia Lottery, the less I like it.

One of the things I like least is the advertising. The General Assembly mandated that lottery advertising must serve the purpose of informing the public about the games, not promoting them. Agreed, that can be a fine distinction, but the current crop of ads seem to step far over that line. Most are undisguised promotion.

"Suppose this is your ticket," the announcer says, rubbing off the latex coating. Apparently it is a winner, because he pockets it, and tries another. "Suppose *this* is your ticket."

This is a straightforward appeal to greed. But the ad contains an underlying honesty its writers probably didn't intend. Chances are good that when you do buy a ticket, it will be that second one--the loser.

The same announcer, in another spot, stands chest deep among stacks and stacks of winning lottery tickets. I suppose lottery officials consider this a method of "informing" us about our chances of winning--without actually encouraging us to rush out and try to get our hands on one of those eleven million tickets. And I suppose that, technically, they'd be right--just like the Miller Brewing Company "informs" us that their product is less filling and tastes great. After all, neither ad is directly asking us to buy anything, right?

But the ad that disturbed me most was one I heard on the radio. In this spot, someone at a check-out counter "just happens" to write a check for a dollar more than the amount of the purchase. Rather than getting change or writing a new check, the customer applies that extra dollar to buy a lottery ticket.

Many new players might feel uneasy about walking up to a clerk for the sole purpose of purchasing a lottery ticket. Whoever is running the lottery recognizes we have to overcome some psychological barriers before we feel comfortable participating. So they cleverly provide a behavioral model for those of us who may be tempted to play, but need to rationalize our behavior. The clerk and other customers aren't going to be looking down on some dissolute gambler buying chances in a sweepstakes, the ad tells us. Instead, they'll see an ordinary citizen who "just happens" to have an extra dollar on hand in the checkout line.

Even worse than the advertisements, however, is what the lottery seems to be doing to some of our citizens. Last week I saw a woman drive up to a convenience store, walk in, and purchase three lottery tickets and a pack of cigarettes. Her rusting car needed new tires and, judging from the blue smoke issuing from the tailpipe, engine repair as well. Her worn clothing made me suspect her wardrobe could have used similar attention. None of her tickets were winners; she threw them in the trash on her way out of the store.

Chances are you won't see the wealthiest Virginian stopping in to play *Money Match* at your local Seven-Eleven. It's people like this woman who buy the tickets. People for whom a thousand dollars, or even a hundred, would make a significant difference in their lives--the very people who can least afford to expend their limited resources on lottery tickets. The irony of the lottery is that people who, proportionally, stand to gain the most from the lottery and who provide the bulk of its financial support, are the ones who can least afford to play and are most harmed by it.

Like it or not, one of government's roles is to redistribute wealth so everyone, rich or poor, receives the services they need. The lottery clearly undermines the principle that those who have the most should shoulder the greatest burden to maintain our society. The wealthy, who could contribute a little more to the common wealth of the Commonwealth will not pay their fair share through the lottery. Instead, the lottery taps the rest of us to fill the treasury. And worse, it does so inefficiently—only thirty-five percent of every dollar collected makes it to the state coffers.

Finally, let's consider Virginians who may be vulnerable to developing addictive behaviors. How many gamblers, who might otherwise have never engaged in their addiction, will be drawn into the game because of its easy availability? We'll never have a precise numerical answer, but there can be no doubt some individuals will play compulsively. Once they begin, they will be unable to stop, even when their finances and their family's wellbeing start to suffer. Such an outcome cannot be justified.

I realize it's not possible to save people from their own weaknesses by rule of law. But at the very least government shouldn't be in the business of leading them to temptation.

For now, it looks like we're stuck with a bad idea. The General Assembly isn't about to give up all that revenue, and most Virginians aren't going to want to give up their chances to hit the jackpot. As with tobacco and alcohol, we're going to have to live with the lottery for a while, despite its unfortunate side effects.

Behavioral psychologists tell us that the most effective way to encourage a behavior is to reward it intermittently. In other words, an occasional five or ten dollar win will keep us buying ticket after ticket. Maybe, once the newness of the lottery wears off and people learn from experience that money spent on lottery tickets is a poor investment, sales will diminish and the harmful effects of the lottery will be minimized. And maybe we'll take another vote someday, and decide that it wasn't such a good idea after all. I'm not counting on it, but I've got my fingers crossed.

Style Weekly, Nov. 22, 1988

A Time to Remember, A Time to Act

August 6 is the 50th anniversary of the bombing of Hiroshima. A bomb from a single U.S. aircraft, the Enola Gay, destroyed a city and killed over 100,000 people that day. Fifty years later our nation still has difficulty taking responsibility for this devastating act against a civilian target. Fifty years later, reasonable people still disagree about why the United States chose to use such a terrible weapon, and whether it was militarily necessary or morally justified.

Did the bombing speed a Japanese surrender and save the lives of U.S. soldiers? History records that the Japanese were already making overtures to negotiate their surrender. Was it a message to Stalin and the Soviet military? Uncertain about whether the new technology would work, President Truman rejected the suggestion that the U.S. stage a demonstration of the weapon at a remote and unpopulated location. What purpose was served by the destruction of Nagasaki three days later, before the Japanese leadership had time to assess the damage from the first bombing?

Most of us have lived our whole lives in the shadow of that 1945 mushroom cloud. Many of us remember "duck and cover" drills in school. Even as young children we understood the absurdity of hiding beneath a desk to protect ourselves from a nuclear fireball.

Through it all, we've had to live as if the threat of

nuclear annihilation didn't exist. To lead sane, productive lives, we've had to push nuclear destruction from our consciousness, lest we become overwhelmed with despair and fear.

But the anniversary of the Hiroshima bombing is a time to remember. August 6 is a time to remember the dead, both Japanese and American. It's a time to marvel at the scientific and technical achievements that built our nuclear arsenal, and to reflect on the awesome power we've placed in the hands of young military men and women barely out of high school. And it's time to remember that nuclear weapons are still with us every day, despite our new political era.

So how do we contain this nuclear danger? First, we must slow or stop further development of nuclear weapons around the world. The Comprehensive Test Ban Treaty, on the table since 1963, can help achieve this end.

The "reliability" of U.S. nuclear weapons can be assessed by non-nuclear means. With current technology a test ban is fully verifiable. A treaty signed by the nuclear powers—along with most other nations—will make it far more difficult for any "near nuclear" nation to proceed with its weapons program and still maintain good relations with the rest of the world.

President Clinton says he supports the treaty. He should instruct his envoys to finish their negotiations immediately and present the final document to Congress and the American people.

Second, we should resume Strategic Arms Reduction

Talks with Russia and the other nuclear powers, with the goal of negotiating much deeper cuts in the world's arsenals. Any rationale for maintaining a huge stock of nuclear warheads has now completely disappeared.

Ten thousand nuclear weapons—the current U.S. nuclear stockpile—provide us no protection against terrorist attacks. They can't prevent unfair international trade practices or keep manufacturing jobs in our country. They don't even give our government leverage in deterring small-scale aggression or settling regional conflicts. Would we use nuclear weapons in Bosnia or Somalia?

The only rationale for maintaining a nuclear arsenal is to counter those other nations who have nuclear weapons of their own. Does that require 10,000 warheads? Do we need the 6,000 we're scheduled to retain when current arms reduction treaties take effect? No. Experts tell us that about 200 nuclear warheads would be enough to effectively destroy all of Russia.

Stockpiling 6,000 weapons buys no additional security. One tenth of our current arsenal would be more than adequate to provide whatever deterrence we may need until the world becomes a safer and more peaceful place.

Every additional nuclear warhead beyond that number increases the possibility of theft, nuclear terrorism, accidental detonation or intentional misuse. Every warhead we dismantle reduces those risks.

Every additional warhead we maintain adds millions of dollars to the federal budget at a time when Congress is struggling with a growing national debt. Nuclear weapons squeeze funds from programs for health, education, social welfare and the arts, as well as conventional military preparedness.

Retaining our own huge nuclear force makes it easier for other nuclear powers to justify enlarging or upgrading their arsenals. France has recently taken just such a step with its decision to resume nuclear testing in the Pacific. A just-completed report by the U.S. Nuclear Weapons Cost Study Project shows that since 1945 our government has spent as much as one-third of the military budget on nuclear arms.

Most important, maintaining a large stock of nuclear weapons encourages other near nuclear nations to join the arms race. Iran, North and South Korea, Taiwan, Japan and several other nations could all become nuclear powers before the turn of the century, making our world far more dangerous and unstable. Only by showing a commitment to reducing the size of our arsenal does the United States gain any diplomatic and political leverage in its efforts to persuade other nations to abandon the nuclear option.

And finally, we must not allow ourselves to forget the nuclear burden that our nation still bears. We may feel safer now than during the Cuban Missile Crisis or the high-tension times of the 1980s, but we're still face great risk. That's worth remembering on August 6…and every day thereafter.

Style Weekly, August 1, 1995

Preserving the ABM Treaty

How does it feel to be a citizen of a "rogue state"?

Since taking office, the Bush administration has brazenly disregarded one international agreement after another. They've opted out of the Kyoto accord on global warming, an international agreement to enforce the ban on biological weapons, and a treaty establishing an International Court of Justice, among others.

Now, as the centerpiece of its policy of doing whatever it chooses, no matter what the rest of the world thinks, the Bush administration has announced it will withdraw from the Anti-ballistic missile (ABM) treaty. According to the text of the treaty, either party can withdraw if "extraordinary events" have "jeopardized its supreme interests." Has that standard been reached in 2001? At best, Bush's plan is extremely premature; at worst, it has the potential to destabilize the world's strategic balance.

Bush's high-handed plans have already angered much of the world, including our closest European allies. Nevertheless, the White House has decided to abrogate an international agreement that has helped hold the arms race in check for thirty years.

Why did the United States and the Soviet Union agree to severely limit the development of anti-ballistic missiles in the first place? What's the problem with ABMs?

Anti-ballistic missiles are inherently destabilizing. In a time of heightened political tension, possessing an ABM system might encourage a nuclear-armed nation to strike first. It would be better, the thinking would go, to destroy most of the enemy's missiles in their silos, and then use ABMs to defend against the few warheads remaining. For that reason, developing an ABM system also has the potential to push a nation's adversaries toward an early first strike, before those ABMs are fully deployed.

It also turns out that building ABMs makes little economic sense. It's far cheaper to counter an ABM system by simply building more nuclear missiles. An ABM system might also be defeated with countermeasures to confuse the interceptors; building enough interceptors to take out both the real warheads and their dummy proxies is prohibitively expensive. And finally, because there is no way to test the effectiveness of an ABM system under actual wartime conditions, its reliability would always be suspect.

For those reasons, the world's nuclear superpowers recognized that ABMs would make the arms race both more dangerous and more expensive. So in 1972 they agreed to forego developing and deploying anti-ballistic missiles. Since then, the treaty has been modified several times by mutual consent. In 1974 the parties allowed one another to establish two ABM sites—later reduced to just one. The Soviets positioned nuclear-armed interceptors to provide some defense for Moscow. The United States deployed interceptor missiles in North Dakota, but that base has long since been decommissioned. More recently, the treaty was modified again to allow the development of theater (shorter-range, tactical) defensive missiles such as the Patriot and THAAD.

According to the Bush administration, the purpose of its proposed national missile defense system (NMD) is to intercept an accidental launch, or a few missiles fired by a "rogue state." This sounds like a reasonable goal. But suppose a small but nuclear-armed nation decided to attack the United States with a nuclear weapon. Would they fire a missile or two—thus offering their country up for fiery retaliation from the only nation ever to have used nuclear weapons in war? Wouldn't it be cheaper, easier and less risky to tuck a warhead inside a cargo ship or rental truck and detonate it anonymously? Star Wars technology isn't much good against a bomb in a crate. A much better defense would be to find peaceful, negotiated accommodations with those nations.

As far as accidental launches are concerned, there are far more effective—and much less costly—means of prevention. President Bush should be commended for his proposal to reduce the size of our nuclear stockpile. Decreasing the number of warheads in the world's atomic arsenals is the easiest way to reduce the likelihood of an accidental launch. Agreeing to lower the missiles' alert status, and removing specific targeting information from their computers would decrease the risk even further.

Still the administration is willing to toss aside a successful treaty. What will they replace it with? A missile defense system that does not yet exist, and will never work perfectly—no matter how advanced our technology becomes.

So far there have been only a handful of tests of this latest incarnation of the Star Wars defense. NMD is designed to hit incoming warheads with small, maneuverable kinetic (non-explosive) guided missiles. The challenge is often aptly compared to "hitting a bullet with a bullet." The most recent test "succeeded" only because the target warhead, following a predetermined trajectory at a predetermined time, broadcast homing signals to the missile sent to destroy it. North Korea or some other adversary is not likely to be so helpful.

National Missile Defense is a very long way from being able to interdict even a single incoming warhead, never mind destroying a weapon that deploys countermeasures such as radar-reflecting chaff or dozens of dummy warheads. We must not rush to discard the ABM treaty unilaterally in favor of a defense that's little more than a fantasy in the minds of the president and a few Air Force generals and weapons contractors.

The ABM treaty is still worth preserving. Rather than scrapping it altogether, leaders around the world are urging the United States and Russia to renegotiate the treaty to permit development of a limited, shared National Missile Defense. Thus far, Bush is disregarding this advice.

Eventually, some form of limited missile defense may prove to be technologically feasible and strategically wise; many defense experts seem to think so. However, if the United States is to pursue this possibility, we must do so not as a solitary "rogue," but only as an international leader in consultation and cooperation with the other nations of the world.

Is a Man's Best Dog

Style Weekly, September 4, 2001

Note the publication date of this piece. Exactly one week later, the country <u>was</u> under attack. Clearly, Bush's proposed NMD system would have been useless in preventing the massive destruction and loss of life perpetrated by a few determined men armed only with box cutters.

A Day in the Life

"The price of corn is going up again," Bixter grumbled. "Bixter, I wish you wouldn't scan the visipress at breakfast," his wife sighed. "You know it's bad for your digestion."

"Sorry, Sweetheart. It's compulsive, I know. The world is going to hell and I just can't help watching."

"But it's so depressing first thing in the morning. Eat your oatmeal, children. You'll be late for school."

The four children chattered as they finished their breakfasts. They picked up school bags and scampered out through the circular entryway, calling their goodbyes as they went.

Mrs. Bixter was particularly proud of these children. They were all doing well in school, and would probably have professional careers in a couple of years. The last group hadn't turned out quite so well. One was making do as a fast food worker, another a sales clerk, and a third as a medical assistant. But two of the boys were just wandering aimlessly, unable to decide what they wanted from life. She suspected that they were using drugs, too.

Her husband was scanning the news again. "Look at these headlines! Drought in the African grainbelt, double digit inflation, famine in India, threats of war. Won't we ever learn?"

"Learn, dear?" She had long ago learned to be tolerant when he was in one of his moods, and let him get the frustration out of his system. She could see that modern society was beset with a multitude of problems just as well as he could. But she didn't see much point to getting upset about it every morning.

"History," he muttered. "Doesn't anyone remember the Old Books? How can we forget how human civilization destroyed itself in the Old Times? Finally, after hundreds of years in the dark ages, we've managed to rebuild. And we're making the same stupid mistakes they made centuries ago! It's hard to believe."

"I guess we haven't handled things as well as we might have," his wife agreed. "Still, we have a pretty good life, dear." She gently nuzzled his cheek.

"I just hope we don't destroy everything before our grandchildren have the chance to enjoy what's left of this planet."

Mrs. Bixter looked at her watch. "Honey, you better run. You'll miss your shuttle."

"Don't worry. The damned thing's always late anyway. Where's my briefcase?"

"By the front hallway, where you left it. Don't forget to wear that new quair of overshoes I bought you yesterday. They're predicting rain."

"Alright, Dear." Bixter pulled the four molded rubber boots over his leather shoes, settled his hat securely between his ears, straightened his whiskers, and nuzzled his wife goodbye.

"Ah, well, another day in the rat race," she heard him mutter to himself, as his long, hairless tail disappeared through the entranceway.

Pothole Economics

Perhaps you've noticed the deteriorating state of Virginia's roadways. It's hard to miss. Driving on many of the Commonwealth's highways has become a bone-rattling exercise in dodging potholes and thudding over temporary patches. Our interstates are lumpy patchworks of concrete and asphalt. Local streets are cracked and cratered. The paint that should safely delineate lanes and road margins has virtually disappeared from many roads. Even Richmond's iconic boulevard, Monument Avenue, is scarred.

It is false economy to try to save government dollars by postponing road repair. Bad roads are expensive. We pay with more frequent visits to tire stores and auto repair shops. We pay with increased accidents and higher insurance premiums. We pay with inefficiency that adds extra minutes to each trip and extra pennies to the cost of every product transported over the highways.

This disrepair is the direct result of state, local and federal reductions in spending on road maintenance. But tight budgets are a symptom, rather than the ultimate cause of the problem. Our Commonwealth is facing a broader problem than potholes. Pitted, crumbling roadways are just one of the more obvious and irritating results of a misguided political attitude towards government and its functions.

Confronted with a crumbling infrastructure, we have

three choices. One option is to learn to live with it. It can be done. People in the Soviet Union spent years surviving poor, crowded housing, chronic shortages of consumer goods, maddeningly slow and inefficient government bureaucracy, and endless lines. We can adapt to similar decrepitude.

A second choice is to fix the problem ourselves, individually. We could each heat up a pot of asphalt on the stove, stir in some gravel, and fill the holes in the street outside our home or business. If we each pitch in, taking responsibility for one little stretch of road, we might all soon be rolling along smoothly again. But such a solution is obviously doomed to fail.

So what does that leave us? Well, government, of course. Fixing potholes is what we have governments for. That, and lots of other things, like putting out fires, catching criminals, installing streetlights, educating children, making sure our food and medicines are safe, judging our disputes, and a thousand other essential tasks we rely on but can't do ourselves. If we want our roads fixed, we'll have to pay for it.

Tax cuts have become the perennial mantra of too many political campaigns. In the upcoming elections, we're likely to hear the same chant again: taxes and "big government" are bad, and tax cuts inherently good. These claims have gotten state and national politicians elected and kept them in office. Candidates who advocate increased taxes are writing their own political obituaries.

Somehow we've forgotten what our civics teacher explained to us in high school—the reasons why we pay taxes in the first place. Taxes allow us to do things collectively that none of us can accomplish individually. Our tax dollars pay to educate all children, whether or not their families can afford a private school. In the long run, educated children build our society. Taxes pay judges, police officers and firefighters. Taxes maintain our public parks. And, of course, taxes pay for the materials, equipment and personnel who maintain our highways and city streets. When politicians are unwilling to levy sufficient taxes, those services and many others suffer.

If we were to pay a little more for those services, would we really get more in return? Tax-cutting politicians try to sell us the line that increased taxes simply result in more government waste. But is it true? A visit to Canada, or any one of a number of European nations demonstrates this claim is false and deceptive. Yes, the Canadians and Swedes pay more in taxes than we do. But in return they get health services for all, better housing for lower income citizens, care for the elderly, well-maintained streets and beautiful public spaces. No doubt some Canadian bureaucrats misspend tax revenue. Sweden probably has some "waste, fraud and abuse." But citizens of countries with higher taxes generally get what they pay for. Unfortunately, so do we.

It takes tax dollars to fill in those potholes. This November, when some politician tries to secure your vote by promising to "hold the line" on taxes or offers yet another tax cut, keep your eyes on the road. If we want a smoothly functioning society, we have to be willing to pay for it.

Style Weekly, Mar. 23, 2005

Restoring the Voting Rights of *All* Virginians

Imagine stepping into the voting booth and be offered just a single choice—one candidate to cast your vote for in each electoral contest. What would it be like to vote in a place where a single group has such a stranglehold on the electoral process that no one even bothers to run in opposition?

Unfortunately, many of us in Virginia experience just that sort of choiceless election. I've been voting in Virginia for more than 30 years. In that time, I don't remember a single opportunity to choose among two or more candidates for House of Delegates or State Senate. I remember only a couple of House of Representative races in which there were both Democratic and Republican contestants. And in the most recent Senate election, all Virginians had a choice of exactly one candidate.

In too many races, one party or the other doesn't even bother to put up a candidate. If just one candidate is running for office, we have no choice. We may as well not vote at all. Is it surprising that most Virginia elections feature such dismal voter turnouts? I can't help thinking this faulty process—maintained by politicians of both parties whose primary interest is to stay in office--actually denies us our voting rights.

Our voting rights were won at great price. Early suffragists were often outcasts in their own communities. During the Civil Rights movement, determined men and women sacrificed their jobs for the right to vote. Their homes were burned to the ground. They went to jail, or were run out of town. Some paid for the vote with their lives. And if we need yet another reminder of how precious the franchise is, think back to the recent images of South Africans following the end of Apartheid, walking for miles and standing for hours in endless lines to cast their ballots. We owe it to ourselves to make sure that when we go to the polls our votes actually mean something.

So how do we make our voting process more closely approach something genuinely democratic? Here are several suggestions that might help.

The first, and easiest step would be to remove the decennial redistricting process from the political arena. The party in power—whoever that may be--draws district lines to protect its incumbents, and isolate the other party's representatives in a minimum number of opposition-dominated districts. We end up with bizarre Gerrymandered districts for the House of Delegates, State Senate, and U. S. House of Representatives. An overwhelming majority of these districts are thus "safe" for the incumbent, discouraging challengers.

Instead of leaving redistricting to the General Assembly, our political leaders should establish a non-partisan redistricting commission. Lieutenant Governor Tim Kaine made this very proposal several years ago, and it's still a good idea. The commission's task would be to create legislative districts that are geographically compact and, as much as possible, demographically sensible. Urban regions would be focused in single districts, for example, represented by a legislator who lives "in the neighborhood." Compare that with our current system, which has Richmond voters split between two Congressional districts spanning the distance from Hampton Roads to the Blue Ridge Mountains.

Second, Virginia's political parties must field candidates in more contests. Not fielding a candidate—even against a strong incumbent--is plain foolishness. Things happen. Candidates fall ill. They occasionally die in mid-campaign, unfortunately. More frequently, they are revealed to have feet of clay. In the 2004 election, 2nd District Representative Edward Schrock withdrew his candidacy fewer than two months before the election. The two-term Congressman unexpectedly retired after revelations that he had sought sexual encounters with other men. With the incumbent out of the race, what had looked like a Republican cakewalk suddenly became a real contest. Schrock's party had to scramble to find a new candidate.

Meanwhile, the Democrats already had an established candidate, David Ashe. Because he had been actively campaigning, this underdog suddenly had a real chance in a solidly Republican district. In the end, Republican Thelma Drake ended up winning a close race. But the Democrats wouldn't have stood a chance had they failed to contest the seat early on, even though the incumbent appeared to have a great advantage.

I do *not* have the personality of a politician—anyone who knows me will quickly confirm this. I would much rather work in my garden, read, or tap on my keyboard than spend my time in endless meetings, shaking hands with potential supporters. In fact, I'd rather do almost *anything* than put myself through that kind of misery.

But a few years ago, I grew so frustrated with repeatedly uncontested elections in my Republican-dominated congressional district that I went so far as to offer myself to the Democrats as a potential candidate. The very first thing I heard from the party chair was, "do you have $125,000 to spend on the campaign?" That was the wrong response. Both major parties need to welcome and encourage prospective candidates, and help them mount their campaigns.

Finally, Virginia should establish public financing of legislative contests. Incumbents have a huge financial advantage. In Virginia, there are no limits to the amount of campaign contributions state candidates and officeholders can accept. Nor are the reports of those contributions to the State Board of Elections audited. Citizens who wish to examine these self-policed disclosures must visit the SBE offices in Richmond, although many legislators now voluntarily post the information on the Virginia Public Access Project website (www.vpap.org).

In order to give potential competitors a running start against an incumbent's huge advantage, the General Assembly should establish a fund available to any candidate who can garner a minimum number of signatures from registered voters in their district.

Public financing would have the added benefit of

enabling independents and third party candidates to mount more credible campaigns--as long as they can demonstrate public support by gathering enough signatures. More candidates--espousing a wider range of viewpoints—will surely energize the electorate and entice more of us to exercise the right to vote. It's a right too precious to be denied us by our own politicians.

Virginia Forum, Feb. 9, 2005

A recent court decision has resulted in more compact Congressional districts in central Virginia. And the idea of a nonpartisan redistricting commission has been floated again in 2014 and 2016, after the most recent elections. A substantial number of national and state organizations—including Common Cause, OneVirginia2021 and others—are now actively campaigning to make it happen. It's still a good idea.

Why Not Raise Taxes on Those Who Can Afford It?

Here's something to think about the next time you visit the library, hear the siren of an ambulance or fire truck, dodge a pothole, or see a yellow bus picking up kids for school: There are lots of good reasons to pay taxes. And here in Virginia, many of us could afford to pay a little more.

Right now the state and its localities are wrestling with budget crises. The pages of this newspaper are filled with daily reports of politicians debating what programs to cut, and citizens begging to keep those programs funded. Despite their protestations of pain, those officials seem too willing to cut programs that citizens value, including public education, extracurricular and after-school activities, recreation programs, health clinics, and even public safety.

We depend on government to provide such services for the benefit of us all. As individuals, we can't supervise our community's teenagers after school—and most of us wouldn't want to. But providing constructive, supervised activities is clearly something we must do in order for our young people to maintain healthy, safe and orderly lives. We can't individually grab a shovel and go out to fill potholes. But we certainly want government to maintain the roads, so we don't blow a tire or break an axle the next time we drive out for groceries. When we dial 911, we expect a government employee to respond— right away. In short, we get a lot of value in return for our tax dollars.

Government spending doesn't make us poorer—it enriches our community. It's called the multiplier effect. When government pays the salary of a teacher or firefighter, we get the benefit of that employee's service. But that salary is also recycled back into the community. Teachers buy groceries and clothing. Firefighters get their cars serviced, and take their families out to dinner. The money they spend pays the owners and employees of the local businesses they patronize, and the producers of the goods those businesses purvey. That money is then passed on again to other businesses and workers. Economists estimate that each additional dollar of expenditure creates about five dollars of economic wealth as it circulates through our community.

As it turns out, many of us in the Commonwealth could actually afford to pay a little more to counteract the shortfall in local and state budgets. Despite the current hard times, plenty of Virginians are still doing well. Virginia is among the top ten states in per capita income. According to recent census data, at least 150,000 Virginia households have incomes greater than $150,000 a year. Such families can afford a modest tax increase.

Virginia still allows wealthy seniors to collect Social Security benefits untaxed. And Virginia—home to some of the nation's largest corporations--has a lower corporate tax rate than all but one other state. Yet astoundingly, some legislators have been calling for the elimination of that minimal tax—an idea we must hope will be laughed out of the General Assembly.

Right now, local and state politicians are tripping over one another as they search for places to cut essential services, while satisfying virtually no one. With a little more courage, our leaders could easily raise additional revenue from those individuals and corporations who can afford to pay a bit more. I for one would willingly support a fair tax increase that would maintain my local park, ensure the neighborhood kids have an adequate education and worthwhile things to do after school, and fill in the potholes that currently make the drive into town a frame-twisting adventure. Perhaps the new administration and General Assembly will have the guts, foresight and civic responsibility to take such a step.

Richmond Times-Dispatch, guest column, Feb.1, 2010

Armed and Unready

A twenty-one foot rented powerboat skims across the waves alongside the Hampton Roads bridge-tunnel. The driver turns his craft towards Norfolk, where three huge aircraft carriers and a number of smaller naval vessels are berthed. He pushes the throttle forward, his bow slamming against the choppy waves.

As he approaches the naval yard, two armed patrol craft sprint out to intercept him. They fire a warning flare, and instruct the craft to turn away. But their warning is much, much too late. With a flick of a switch, the powerboat disappears in a ten million degree flash of heat and light. In an instant, a quarter of the U.S. Atlantic fleet is vaporized, and 100,000 Virginians are dead or dying. Thousands more are seriously injured, dispossessed or condemned to premature death from cancer. And an entire nation is thrown into panic as millions try to flee the cities in fear of other possible attacks.

Such a catastrophe is unimaginable. But we must focus our imaginations on it if we are to have any hope of preventing it. As former assistant secretary of defense Graham Allison points out in his book *Nuclear Terrorism*, all other terrorist threats pale in comparison to the danger posed by a nuclear attack.

A nuclear weapon capable of destroying Hampton Roads or Richmond or Northern Virginia could weigh as little as two hundred pounds. It could fit in a large suitcase or backpack. The former Soviet Union built thousands of such weapons. Many of them are still not secured, or even accounted for.

Terrorists who wished to build their own bomb instead could develop plans from information freely available in the world's libraries or on the internet. They would need to acquire just nine pounds of plutonium, an amount about the size of a softball. A slightly larger amount of highly enriched uranium would also serve, and would be much easier to obtain and work with. These bomb-making materials are readily available in dozens of countries with loosely guarded nuclear power reactors.

Once terrorists have purchased, stolen or built a nuclear bomb, preventing them from smuggling it into the country and using it to destroy a U.S. target is much more difficult. Every year smugglers transport thousands of tons of illegal drugs and other contraband across our borders. We can't even manage to interdict the hundreds of thousands of immigrants entering our country without documentation. How difficult would it be to transport a bomb that could easily fit in the trunk of a car or a large suitcase? Radiation sensors are virtually useless against such a weapon. A properly shielded nuclear bomb releases almost no detectable radiation.

So what can be done to prevent this scenario from becoming a tragic reality? Allison proposes a comprehensive, coordinated program. It includes preventing additional nations from acquiring nuclear weapons or the capacity to produce weapons-grade uranium and plutonium, building an international alliance to deter nuclear terrorism, and rewarding both friends and adversaries for their cooperation. The plan also includes meeting our nation's treaty commitments to reduce our own nuclear arsenal. We cannot successfully call on other countries to disarm unless we ourselves take genuine steps in that same direction.

The centerpiece of Allison's proposal calls for safeguarding nuclear warheads currently spread across Russia, and securing or removing the highly enriched uranium and plutonium now resident in dozens of countries with nuclear power reactors. It's a step we must take immediately.

There is already a program, created during the administration of the first President Bush by Senators Richard Lugar and Sam Nunn, intended to accomplish just that. It has been enormously successful in securing and dismantling nuclear weapons from the states of the former Soviet Union. But the job is only half completed. The Nunn-Lugar program is grossly underfunded, and the current Bush administration has not pushed for its rapid completion.

This is where Virginia's congressional delegation can make a great difference. A nuclear terror attack may still be preventable, if we take immediate steps to make unsecured bombs and bomb-making material unavailable at its source. The Commonwealth's representatives and senators should support appropriations to fund the rapid completion of the Nunn-Lugar program. We must help Russia secure its remaining nuclear weapons, plutonium and highly-enriched uranium to what Allison calls the "gold standard"—that is, making them as secure as the gold in Fort Knox.

Allison estimates this task will cost about 30 billion dollars. Is there money to carry it out? There must be.

Imagine the economic disaster that would face our country if a single bomb were detonated in an American city. For starters, let's redirect some of the billions the Bush administration is now pouring into its high tech "missile shield," a defense that will be marginally effective at best against a minimal attack by long-range missiles. That's clearly not where the gravest danger lies.

Sixty years ago the United States became the first and only nation to use nuclear weapons against another country. Since then the world has managed to avoid the horrors of another nuclear blast. If we are to continue that good fortune, and avoid having our own terrible invention used against us, our government must do everything in its power to help the world lock down its nuclear fuel and weapons.

Style Weekly, February 16, 2005

Why Loving Matters

In 1973 I moved to Richmond for grad school, and met my future wife. It was love at first sight, or pretty damn close-- at least on my part. And so we began a relationship that would have been illegal only a few years earlier. The U.S. Supreme Court's 1967 *Loving* decision had recently declared Virginia's anti-miscegenation statute to be unconstitutional. People of different "races" could legally marry – which Debra (of African ancestry) and I (European) did in 1975.

The current cases before the Court seeking recognition for same-sex marriages remind us of that earlier decision. And of course, like laws banning race-mixing, prohibiting same sex unions ignores thousands of years of actual human behavior.

"Interracial" dating and marriage is now so ordinary that for all but die-hard segregationists, it has become almost entirely unremarkable—Although I admit Debra and I still feel pleased when we see "mixed" families featured in television commercials or encounter multiracial couples and their children on the street. However, we experienced *much* less acceptance in mid-1970s Virginia.

We didn't know any other couples in our situation. Cashiers assumed we were separate customers when we stood in the supermarket checkout line. Restaurant hosts didn't know what to do with us. People stared when we were out in public. Once, in a mall parking lot, an entire (white, of course) family walked directly into a parked car as they turned to gawk. We had no shortage of such episodes to amuse us.

Debra's family welcomed me into their midst with amazing openness, although her parents surely wondered whether she was making the right choice. Becoming part of their family and community has enriched my life beyond measure. I think their generosity is the greatest gift I have ever received.

Debra felt welcomed into my family as well, although I doubt that would surprise anyone who knows her – like her late father she has the ability and inclination to instantaneously befriend almost anyone.

I don't want to make light of the challenges we faced, *Loving* notwithstanding. There were some places – Colonial Heights, for example – we transited with care or avoided whenever possible. When we drove south for a Florida vacation, Debra's parents worried for our safety, and we took precautions other travelers might not.

It was very difficult for us to find a real estate agent willing to help us find our first home. Our marriage limited Debra's opportunities for professional advancement throughout her entire career. And we don't fool ourselves into thinking that the bitter remnants of racism and inequality are not *still* with us every day.

Attitudes towards interracial marriage have changed slowly, but what once was socially unacceptable has become commonplace. Public acceptance of marriage equality for gay and lesbian couples is clearly on that same path, no matter what the U.S. Supreme Court may decide later this month.

ACLU of Virginia Blog, 2015

A Friend in Need

Verse

Ephemera

Early November, late afternoon.
In a southern corner, sheltered from the wind
Tiny bits of winged fluff
Golden in the lowering sun
Dart, float,
Swirl in a living vortex
Rising, falling
Finding one another
In the waning afternoon.
Dancing, mating, dying
As the sun slips behind the trees
And the long, cold night begins.

Stopped by Weeds on a Summer Morning

Whose weeds these are I'm sure I know.
I've watched them as they sprout and grow.
No time to rest or sip a beer—
I better run and grab my hoe.

My little garden slowly clears
of undergrowth. I persevere.
My fingers blister; shoulders ache
This longest evening of the year.

I give my aching arms a shake,
lean on my hoe to take a break.
What drudgery it is to reap
This loathsome crop, for goodness sake.

I strike each weed a killing blow
knowing more will soon regrow.
It is the gardener's *quid pro quo*...
Those miles of rows to rake and hoe.

Is a Man's Best Dog

This is Just to Say

    by William Carlos Squirrel

This is just to say
I have eaten
the corn
that you planted
in the garden

and which
you were probably
planning to pick
for dinner.

It was delicious,
so sweet and so crisp.

And soon
the tomatoes
will turn
as red as your wheelbarrow.

The Alternative Gourmet

You may eat each pea with a knife and honey
If such is your chosen habit.
But I prefer using a sharp-pronged fork
And trying my damnedest to stab it.

They Said It Couldn't Be Done

A flavorful drink can be fashioned
By squeezing an orange in
An icy cold glass of domestic
Or excellent foreign gin.

Rhinoceros

I don't believe I've ever seen a rhinoceros like you.
Instead of having one horn, you insist on wearing two.
The one and only thing you ever say to me is "moo."
It's no wonder why no other rhinos dine with you!

The English Are a Funny Language, Amn't It?

An angler developed a cough
While standing all day in a slough.
He said that although
He stood under a bough,
Its protection just wasn't enough.

Cephalopods

Cephalopods

Have their feet on their heads.

When you think they're arriving,

They're leaving instead.

The Onion

The onion is blessed with a spirit

That carrots or celery lack.

You have to admire a vegetable

With the wherewithal to bite back.

Nature, Red in Tooth and Claw

A buzzard ate a lizard
Which stuck inside his gizzard
So he went to see a wizard,
Stunned with suffering and doubt.

The wizard said, "A lizard
In the gizzard is a hazard,"
So he mustered up his courage,
Reached within and pulled it out.

The lizard was quite flustered,
In a tizzy, feeling drowsy.
He muttered, "Just like Lazarus
I've risen from the dead."

The other buzzards clustered
Like a blizzard 'round their cousin.
"Next time stick to custard,"
The other buzzards said.

New Jersey Turnpike

Asphalt and stone
Ripped from the earth and inverted.
Black, sticky rich, Earth inside out.

No ribbon,
This intransient girdle of Earth's own substance
Drawn, too tight, by her own children.

Quadriplegic—Vietnam 1968

Each heartbeat an indictment.
Each outward breath a prayer.
Each inward, a curse.

Hopewell, Virginia

Capture this city in a mayonnaise jar.
Unscrew the lid
And let Hopewell fill the room.

The sun filters red through smoke and vapor.
Dank clouds hover above low rooftops,
Twisted and purple in the morning light.
A slick gray residue collects on windowpanes.
Acrid fumes catch at the back of the throat.
The taste lingers.

The river flows dark and oily,
Sticky brown scum collects on old bottles
And plastic cups lining the bank.
Delicate morning mist rises from the water
Gently lifting the odors of chemicals and decay.

At the city line, a sign proudly read
"Chemical Capital of the South."
The sign is gone now.
The pride is gone now.
The clinging, corrosive mists remain.

We want to put Hopewell back into the
      mayonnaise jar.
But we don't know how.

Dayenu

The sun warms a single blade of grass.
It grows.
This one event
confirms this planet
as a place of miracles.

The world is covered
with a thin, fragile film of life.
Yet more amazing, this life is aware,
and aware of itself, amazed.

Still, on some tomorrow,
the warming sun will contract, gasp and expand,
leaving nothing but a glowing cinder
where a world of miracles had once been.

November Evening

On a darkening November evening
Wind swirls the fallen leaves.
They rush like phantom birds
Fleeing the onslaught of a storm.

Spring Breeze

A spring breeze drifts through the branches
Oak blossoms quiver.
Pollen drifts downward in yellow streamers
Onto a still, shallow puddle.
It floats on the oily surface,
Collecting in bright streaks, yellow on black.
Reflections of white clouds in a blue sky
Disappear into the damp gravel
At the water's edge.

Leftovers

The Herring are Running, the Herring are Running

Every spring, up the tributaries of the Atlantic from Florida to Nova Scotia, they come by the millions to spawn. Silver flashes break the surface in a thousand fresh-water streams. Small schools of fish dart up the swiftly flowing waters with surprising speed, then circle and rest in quiet backwaters before dashing upstream again.

All along the Atlantic coast, the annual herring runs signal the coming of summer just as surely as the new growth on trees. Fishers gather on the banks of creeks, wielding oversized dip nets to harvest the silvery fish. Herring certainly can't be considered a sport fish, but the runs provide a pleasant, sociable, productive way to spend an afternoon. Those of us who live near streams where herring spawn--many of which are eponymously named Herring Run or Herring Creek--wouldn't miss this yearly opportunity for good fun and good eating.

River herring, as they are known, are actually two different species with very similar appearance. The more common is *Alosa pseudoharengus*, also known as the alewife. The other is *Alosa aestivalis*, or the blueback herring. Both species have dozens of other common names, varying from locality to locality. Telling the two species apart using external characteristics is difficult; the only obvious difference is that the alewife has a somewhat larger eye. Internally, they are easily distinguished. The peritoneum--the membrane lining the body cavity--of the alewife is pinkish, while that of the blueback herring is black.

In both species the females tend to be slightly larger than the males. Of course in spawning season the males bear large white sacs of milt, and the females carry their golden treasure of roe.

River herring weigh about half a pound each. They have blue-green backs and silvery sides covered with large, loose scales. Their tails are deeply forked, the mark of a swift swimmer. Their belly is roughened and serrated from gills to vent, giving rise to one common name--sawbelly.

Like salmon, river herring are anadromous, spending part of their lives in fresh water and part in salt. Spawned and hatched far up in fresh water streams, the young swim downstream to the Atlantic in late summer or fall. Those that survive the dangers of that journey and their ocean life return to fresh water as adults to spawn three or four years later. Biologists don't yet know whether, like salmon, herring return to the stream of their birth. But they suspect the fish at least return to the same general region.

Unlike salmon, herring don't die after spawning. They return to the sea and may spawn several times in their adult lives. These toothless plankton-feeders depend for survival on sheer numbers, traveling in huge schools during their life in the ocean, and making their spawning journeys in groups as well.

Native Americans on the Atlantic coast depended on river herring as an important source of protein. In the early days of our country European settlers also depended on them, especially preserved with salt and used for sustenance during the lean winter months. Colonists marveled at the abundance of these fish and their larger cousins, the shad. Unfortunately, the damming of many coastal rivers and streams, and heavy commercial fishing has drastically reduced contemporary herring populations. But the fish are still abundant in some of our coastal streams.

Commercial fishers catch herring by the ton in fish pounds, traps and seines. Most of the catch is used to make fish meal for animal feed. For the amateur, the most common method for taking them is dipping them out of the water with a long-handled, wide-mouthed dip net. These nets are best outfitted with a mesh of chicken wire rather than twine. This allows the net to remain open whether it's facing upstream or downstream.

There are two prime locations for dipping in a stream when the fish are running. One is a deep hole where the herring congregate and rest before resuming their migration. The other is any place in the stream where the water surges through a deep channel in an otherwise shallow or narrow section. The fish tend to stay in the channels and deeps as they dart up the creeks.

Fishers often work a creek in teams. One handles the net while another, starting some distance downstream, noisily wades toward the net, beating the water with a stick and running the fish before him. If nothing else, this makes for great fun on a warm spring afternoon. On a good day, in the right location, it's not uncommon to catch more than a gallon of fish in a single dip.

There are other methods of taking herring as well. Give the right topography, it's possible to catch them in a seine or even a cast net. Herring will not take either live bait or most lures--they are plankton feeders after all. But they will sometimes hit a shad dart retrieved through the water with a series of short jerks. However, if the object is to catch a lot of fish, this method is both unreliable and highly inefficient.

You sometimes see people fishing for herring with snatch hooks, bare, weighted treble hooks which are jerked though the water, snagging fish on their barbed points. This is a brutal, unsportsmanlike method that undoubtedly leaves many wounded fish in the water, torn but uncaught.

The laws regulating herring fishing vary from place to place. For example, a special county license is required for dip-netting in my home state of Virginia. Any local sporting goods or bait store should have the information you need to be a legal angler. They should also be able to suggest when to expect the herring to run. In Virginia, the heaviest runs begin around the end of April, and last for over a month. Timing of the runs will vary, of course, as you travel north or south.

Many people use herring as live bait to troll for bluefish or striped bass. I've even met someone in Rhode Island who follows the tradition taught to the Pilgrims by Native

Americans. He drops one or two of these abundant little fish into each hill of corn he plants, as fertilizer. I suppose this would also be a wise way to dispose of the heads and entrails. I sometimes save some of the heads in the freezer to use as crab bait later in the summer.

Once you've caught a bucketful of fish, you'll face what will appear to be a monumental cleaning task. It's not nearly as bad as it looks. Herring can be cleaned quickly and easily. The large, loose scales come off rapidly as long as the fish have been kept wet. After that, cut off the head just behind the gills. The reproductive organs should then be visible in the body cavity.

If the fish is a female, carefully make a slit along the belly to the vent so as not to damage the roe. Save the two golden sacs of eggs and discard the rest of the viscera. The males can be cleaned with less care. Simply lay the fish on its side, slice off the lower "sawbelly" part of the fist to the vent, and remove the entrails.

To complete the cleaning, strip out the membrane that lines the body cavity. Hold the fish under running water and run your thumb along the underside of the backbone to remove the blood as you rinse.

Unfortunately, fresh herring is barely edible. It's not that the meat doesn't taste good; in fact it's delicious. But these little fish are laced with hundreds of tiny bones that make eating them extremely tedious. Nevertheless, I do know a number of people who hold a different opinion; they pan-fry their fresh herring in butter and tackle the arduous task of eating around the bones with great pleasure.

Fresh herring roe is a delicacy many people find superior to the coarser, more expensive roe harvested from shad. Herring roe is easy to prepare. Simply sauté it in butter. Or dip the sacs of roe in beaten egg, and then dredge in salted and peppered flour, cornmeal or cracker crumbs. The breaded roe can then be pan fried or quickly deep fried. The roe cooks fast and should not be allowed to dry out with overcooking. Serve with lemon wedges, tartar sauce and crisp strips of bacon.

Salted or pickled herring is a taste treat you can enjoy months after the last fish has spawned and returned to the ocean. To pickle herring, thoroughly clean the fish as described above. Cut them across the backbone into steaks about one inch thick. Cover the steaks with brine made from two cups of non-iodized salt per gallon of water, and refrigerate for two or three days. This brining firms up the flesh.

After the fish has soaked in brine, rinse thoroughly. In glass jars, alternate layers of fish with slices of fresh onion. Add a bay leaf or two and sprinkle in a few peppercorns, mustard seeds, dill seeds and whole allspice. Cover the fish completely with a pickling solution made of equal parts of white or wine vinegar and water. Store in the refrigerator. The herring will be ready to eat in two to three weeks, and will keep perfectly well in the refrigerator for months.

Here's how to salt herring, courtesy of Dick Cook of the Virginia Sea Grant Marine Advisory service: Split the cleaned fish lengthwise, cutting through the ribcage along one side of the backbone. Wash the fish thoroughly. In a stone or pottery crock or large glass container, lay down an inch of non-iodized salt. Then alternate single layers of fish and salt, making sure the salt covers each piece of fish completely on all sides. Leave another inch of salt at the top of the container, and store in a cool, dark place.

After five days, check the container. There should be brine at the top, from the liquids the salt has drawn from the fish. Dip out the brine and top off the crock with more salt. After about six weeks your salt herring should be ready to eat. Kept in a cool, dark place, the salt fish should stay preserved for a year or more.

To prepare salt herring, remove the amount of fish you need from the container and rinse. Soak the fish for about four hours in fresh water, rinse, and soak again. To cook the fish, just roll it in cracker crumbs or cornmeal and pan fry.

The great advantage to preserving herring before it is eaten is that, especially when pickled, the bones soften and become almost unnoticeable. These preparations are not as difficult or time consuming as they may sound. In addition to the fun of an afternoon spent catching these silvery fish, the end results of your efforts will be, in a word, delicious.

Farmstead, Spring 1980

Unfortunately, the herring runs I wrote about have all but disappeared on the James River and its tributaries. However, as a result of conservation efforts, including restocking and dam removals, spring shad runs in the James have been making a slow comeback. I hope their cousins the herring will return as well.

I've included this one example from among a number of "how to" pieces written early in my writing career. Many magazines seemed eager for step-by-step explications detailing how to do almost anything. (Around that time, I remember <u>Playboy</u> running an article--not mine, unfortunately--about how to shave! The author of that piece probably earned a thousand dollars for his efforts.)

My own articles included pieces on how to catch and cook crabs, gather and prepare mussels, support garden plants on trellises, teach spelling skills to children creatively, as well as how to teach kids to create code to produce simple computer graphics on Apple II computers.

Writing these pieces helped me develop both fluency and the confidence that I could write well enough that someone would be willing to publish my words, and, even better, pay me a little something for the work.

Reviews

Claiming Georgia Tate

by Gigi Amateau

Georgia Tate is a twelve year old with more trouble than any adolescent should have to bear. When we first meet this motherless child, she is living with her grandparents in a small Mississippi town. When her grandmother dies unexpectedly, Georgia Tate is sent to Florida to live with her father, where she endures both deprivation and sexual abuse.

Richmonder Gigi Amateau's tells Georgia Tate's story in the first person, present tense. Her writing perfectly captures the slow-paced, family- and church-centered life of the rural South. Through most of this debut novel, Georgia Tate's clear, pure voice rings with a genuine combination of youthful innocence and wisdom.

The second part of the novel takes something of a detour. Amateau introduces a series of multi-cultural characters, including a Haitian immigrant grandmother, a cross-dressing cosmetologist and a hulking Black ex-convict who writes poetry. None of them are fully realized; rather these characters all seem intended to teach us that goodness and decency can be found in many kinds of people. Not even the abusive, drunken father comes alive in quite the way that Georgia Tate and her grandparents do earlier in the story. However, toward the end of the novel Amateau once again finds her protagonist's voice, as Georgia Tate begins the process of rebuilding her shattered life.

Claiming Georgia Tate is written for young adult readers. Because this short novel includes scenes of incestuous abuse and some harsh language, it is likely to generate controversy. Amateau herself recommends that adolescents read the novel with parental guidance and discussion. That's probably good advice.

Although *Claiming Georgia Tate* tells a grim tale, young readers and their parents will admire its heroine's courage and strength in the face of her terrible trials. And readers will love the enchanting, evocative language Amateau uses to bring this plucky young woman to life. Georgia Tate is one of those rare literary characters who stays with you long after you turn the final page.

State of Fear

by Michael Crichton

Michael Crichton has his doubts about global warming. Unfortunately, instead of explaining his reservations in a short essay, he decided to incorporate them into a ponderous 560-page novel, complete with bibliography.

When he's at his best, Crichton's techno-thrillers are fast-paced and scientifically plausible. But *State of Fear* doesn't come close to meeting the standards he set in earlier novels like *The Andromeda Strain* and *Jurassic Park*.

Crichton's current offering tells the improbable story of an environmental organization gone bad. Unable to capture public support for its campaign against global warming, its directors hatch a plot to convince the world by manufacturing their own ecological disasters around the globe, while ruthlessly murdering anyone who gets in their way.

 The only thing standing in the way of this plot to create havoc with hurricanes, floods and tsunamis are an unlikely band of globe-hopping adventurers. They include a couple of shadowy government agents, a personal assistant who just happens to be a deadly martial artist, an aging philanthropist and his lawyer—the one-dimensional protagonist of the story. Crichton never manages to breathe life into any of his characters, not even his villains. The one character most central to the plot—Kenner, the secret agent--drops in and out of the story without any details about just how he's managing to stay one step behind the bad guys.

 Meanwhile, the plot takes on the flavor of *The Perils of Pauline*. Crichton's heroes fly around the world in an effort to avert one catastrophe after another. Along the way they must evade death by poisonous octopus, flash flood, and burial in an Antarctic glacier. They are even attacked by bolt after bolt of lightning, somehow attracted from the clouds by a tiny--and totally unexplained--electronic device. Far too often Crichton attempts to induce suspense simply by having one character tell the others that he'll have to explain what's going on later.

 Mostly the plot serves as a vehicle for a series of extended lectures--presented clumsily as dialogue—

questioning the legitimacy of the theory of global warming and warning against politicizing pure scientific inquiry.

Crichton has obviously researched his subject carefully. His polemics are carefully referenced to evidence from experimental studies. According to what he's found, the world may not actually be experiencing a global rise in temperatures due to the greenhouse effect, despite what the popular media and public opinion may think. Perhaps Crichton has a point. But readers--and novelists--should be very wary of fiction bearing footnotes.

Electric Dreams,

by Caroline Kettlewell

In 1995, two determined high school teachers recruited a rag-tag bunch of kids from one of the poorest counties in eastern North Carolina and set them on the task of building an electric car. The team—a multi-ethnic mix of academic achievers and shop rats, both male and female--starts with little funding and even less knowledge. The goal: design and assemble a working vehicle and get it to Richmond International Raceway for a regional competition sponsored by Virginia Power.

The kids manage to find an old Ford Escort, which they promptly gut. They have six months to plan how to convert their junker, raise the $10,000 needed to do the job, find a motor, batteries and other parts, install everything and make sure it all works, make the vehicle look presentable and get it to the track. And if they manage to get that far, the team must then compete against wealthy suburban schools from Richmond, northern Virginia and the Carolina research triangle. Will they make it from their rural backwater to the big-time competition at RIR? Does Carolina have barbeque?

Richmond writer Caroline Kettlewell has a fine eye for the details of North Carolina's countryside and its slow, laid-back small town life. Her narrative centers on teachers Harold Miller and Eric Ryan. Ryan is an enthusiastic young Californian, a second-year Teach for America science instructor; Miller is a garrulous, easygoing technology education veteran with a longstanding vision of a future free from internal combustion engines. This mismatched pair complement one another as they push students to tackle a problem far beyond anything previously attempted in their school district. In the process, kids initially skeptical about the project and their chances of completing it come to believe in their abilities, and in the possibilities the world has to offer.

Kettlewell reminds us too often that the Carolina team is an economically disadvantaged underdog. To her great credit, however, she never makes an issue of individual team members' skin color, academic track or GPA, unless it's of particular relevance to the narrative.

Electric Dreams makes it clear that standardized multiple-choice tests are not the sole measure of scholastic excellence. Kids need opportunities to participate in real problem solving, through projects that challenge them to develop and extend their skills. Kettlewell has given us an inspiring alternative vision of what good education can be.

Leading the Resistance—*Come August, Come Freedom: The Bellows, the Gallows and the Black General Gabriel*

by Gigi Amateau

One of the least-known stories from our nation's history is that of the widespread Black resistance to enslavement. From the very beginnings of European settlement of the new world, Africans and their descendants fought against the cruelties of slavery with every means available to them: work slowdowns and sabotage; escape from plantations to native settlements or communities of free Maroons hidden in the wilderness; and even desperate acts of suicide and infanticide.

Young Americans of all racial and ethnic backgrounds need to hear these stories, to gain a more complete understanding of our shared history as well as the current state of our union. Richmond author Gigi Amateau has taken on this task with her new historical novel for young people, *Come August, Come Freedom*. Amateau tells the story of the enslaved Gabriel, who lived just outside Richmond, Virginia. Gabriel, a skilled blacksmith, learned to read and write as a child. As a young man, he was inspired by stories of the American patriots who had recently rebelled against the

English king, as well as contemporary reports of the Black general Toussaint L'Ouverture and his successful revolution against the French slavemasters of Haiti.

In 1800, with the support of his beloved Nan and a small core of family members and others from neighboring farms, Gabriel planned a daring armed rebellion to win freedom. He secretly began forging swords and other weapons. He and his followers would seize arms from local armories, capture Virginia's governor, James Monroe, and demand freedom for the enslaved people of Virginia. Their motto was "Death or Liberty."

His smithy's craft enabled Gabriel to move throughout central Virginia, as he "hired out" to various farms and plantations. As he traveled, he recruited people to his cause. Eventually, hundreds of recruits were ready to follow him. Gabriel believed poor whites and Native Americans would also join the rebellion once it began. Had it not been for the confusion created by torrential rain and flooding on the assigned day of the revolt, Gabriel's scheme might very well have succeeded. Instead, the plan was postponed and then betrayed. More than two dozen of the plotters, including Gabriel himself, were captured and hanged.

Amateau imagines Gabriel's life from infancy through its violent end. Her storytelling is historically accurate and detailed. Much of the book centers on Gabriel's love for Nan, a worker enslaved at a neighboring plantation. These sections provide the deepest glimpse into Gabriel as a person. Unfortunately, there is almost no remaining record of his actual words. Gabriel must surely have been a powerful, charismatic leader, but Amateau imagines less of this aspect of his character than we might like.

Although she is writing for young people, Amateau doesn't hide the horrors of slavery. The story she tells includes beatings and floggings, the hunger and deprivation enslaved people were forced to endure, the sale and separation of families, and even references to slave breeding and the threat of rape by white slaveholders. Her story will help young readers understand that surviving such abuse was a regular part of the lives of enslaved people. Amateau chooses her words carefully—for example, she rarely uses the term *slave* but rather identifies Africans as *the people* or *bondsmen*.

Although Gabriel and Nan's story is brutal and tragic, Amateau manages to tell it in terms suitable for adolescent readers—at least those willing to face the painful facts of our nation's history. Historical documents—some authentic, some imagined—interspersed throughout the text help complete the story. And her writing turns lyrical at times, as she describes the natural beauties of the James River, and the hills and fields where the enslaved people find respite.

Come August, Come Freedom tells an important American story, in an honest and uncompromising way that will touch the hearts and open the eyes of many young readers. Amateau's new novel should generate some challenging, and much needed discussions in our country's living rooms and classrooms.

Rush Hour

I imagine we each have a few indelible memories that simply don't fade, no matter how much we'd prefer never to think of them again. This is one of mine—something to ponder as we head into a new year.

No long ago I was driving home from work on a brisk, clear fall day. The road I travel is a two-lane highway that winds through the countryside southeast of Richmond. As usual on weekday afternoons, there was plenty of traffic.

I saw brake lights flash as the cars ahead of me slowed to a crawl. I was puzzled, because there didn't seem to be any reason to stop. There was no intersection, and not even a driveway, although several houses did sit well back from the highway. As I got closer I could see something moving in the center of the highway, while a steady stream of cars slowly steered around it. A dog in the road, I thought.

And then I could see it wasn't a dog. It was a child. A brown baby in a diaper and white t-shirt was toddling down the yellow center stripe of the road.

Carefully, one by one, the cars and pickups slowly maneuvered past the child, and then sped on their way. No one stopped. Four or five cars had eased past the baby and driven off by the time I got close enough to get a good look at what was happening. I was certain someone would stop and rescue the toddler. But no one did.

Fortunately, there wasn't much traffic in the opposite directions, but what little there was moved along at full speed. My heart was racing. I couldn't quite believe what I was seeing. Would someone grab the baby before it wandered in front of a speeding car? Wasn't anyone going to stop?

The car ahead of me pulled past the child and drove on. The toddler was bawling and teetering unsteadily along the yellow center line. I snapped on my emergency flashers and braked to a stop. I slammed the transmission into park, snatched at the door latch of my car and rushed onto the pavement. I ran to the baby and scooped him up in my arms. A blue pickup sped past us in the other direction, toward Richmond.

In the meantime, a line of cars had backed up behind my little white Toyota. After the truck roared past, they began to swing around my car into the opposite lane, heading on their way.

Up to this point, I really hadn't had much time to think. I was standing in the middle of a busy highway with someone's crying child in my arms. I had no idea where he had come from or where I might find his parents. I don't feel entirely confident managing babies under the best of circumstances. I held the child and tried to comfort him. I asked him his name, but all he did was look at me uncomprehendingly, and cry some more. Clearly I wasn't going to get any information that might help me discover where he belonged.

After the traffic cleared, I walked to the side of the road

and looked in both directions. The nearest house was at least fifty yards away. Too far, it seemed, for a child who could barely walk to have traveled on his own. I didn't see any other clues to suggest where the toddler had come from. I wondered what to do next. I considered driving about half a mile back to the local general store to see if anyone recognized the baby. I could call the police from there, if no one knew him. I decided to inquire at one of the nearest houses first.

I was just about to pull my Corolla onto the shoulder and begin searching when a car squealed to a halt beside me. A young woman jumped out from behind the wheel. "My God," she cried, "Where did you find him?" I told her. The child reached his arms out to her immediately. She took him from me and hugged him; he immediately quieted.

"In the middle of the road?" she asked incredulously. "James said he was going to watch him. That . . . What was he thinking about? I'll kill him when I get home. Oh, my baby! Thank you." She carried the child back to her car, and drove away.

I drove home, shakily, still finding the entire sequence of events difficult to believe. A line of cars swerves to avoid a helpless toddler in the road, yet no one stops to rescue him? What could possibly explain this kind of calloused behavior? I couldn't get it out of my mind, and I still can't.

I know racism was likely a major factor in my neighbors' behavior. I'm still angry each time I picture those cars driving past the child, as if they were trying not to hit a stray dog. Would a white baby have been left in the road by white drivers, the way that Black baby was? Still I can't be sure that the drivers who passed that child by were white, either.

Perhaps our streamlined technology so insulates and isolates us from one another that even the powerful stimulus of a child in distress doesn't penetrate to elicit a protective human response. Yet we sit in front of our televisions, enthralled by the unfolding drama as dozens of people work to rescue a child from a well, 2000 miles away.

This didn't happen in the bustling, anonymous center of some huge metropolis either. This happened in a rural community, where many people, Black and white, have known one another for years. Are we so self-centered and alienated from our fellow humans that we won't even stop to rescue a helpless child? Are we really in that much of a hurry? What about the parents? How could they be so negligent as to allow an unattended toddler to wander onto a busy highway at rush hour? And what about me? Did I do everything I should have done to ensure the child's safety? Probably not. I didn't even think to get the mother's name, and surely I should have.

No matter how I looked at it, the whole event said nothing good about humankind. It still makes me wonder how much of a fool I've been for spending my life teaching children, and doing what little I can to promote a more just and peaceful world. I try to help students learn to accept, respect and understand one another. I try to encourage my fellow humans to throw off the deadly threat of nuclear weapons and live with one another despite our differences. In darker moments, this incident makes those efforts seem pointless.

But I also remind myself that, despite our faults, we're all we've got. The people behind me on the highway saw me stop to help. Maybe they'll stop too, the next time the opportunity to help someone arises.

I travel past that same spot on the highway every day, and I often recall the fleeting events I've just recounted. They remind me how much more we have to learn if we're going to survive and prosper on this planet.

Style Weekly, January 12, 1988

A published comment from one reader of this piece suggested I had made the whole thing up. Afraid not. This really happened.

All that Glitters

Several months ago, the 1988 Winter Olympics concluded in Calgary. Now we're about to be treated to the much grander spectacle of the Summer Games in Seoul, South Korea. Thousands of the world's finest athletes, each at the peak of his or her ability, will meet and compete for the highest honor an athlete can aspire to—Olympic gold.

Unfortunately the Olympic Games have also become a golden opportunity for American broadcasters and journalists to revel in an orgy of narrow, nationalistic reporting. If NBC's sportscasters follow the chauvinistic precedents set by ABC, we can expect to see and hear a great deal this summer about how U.S. athletes are faring. We will find out a great deal less about the achievements of the *best* athletes in each sport, if those athletes happen to be from some other nation.

We can also expect complaints about biased international judging and plenty of breast-beating because our athletes compete without the advantage of financial support from our government. U.S. athletes will even be portrayed as underdogs! (Would anyone be willing to swap Carl Lewis, Willie Banks, Edwin Moses, Florence Griffith, and Jackie Joyner-Kersee et. al. for some other country's track team?)

Our reporters need to take a broader view. In contrast to the border wars, religious strife, economic rivalries and global tension that characterize life as usual on our planet, the

Olympics reflect an all-too-rare spirit of fellowship and cooperation among nations. The Games allow us to set aside our disagreements and honor some spectacular human achievements. When we focus on the U.S. medal count or disregard the efforts of athletes from other nations, we greatly diminish the significance of our athletes' accomplishments and the meaning of the Olympic Games themselves.

Jesse Owens's great performance at the 1936 Berlin Games meant far more than four gold medals for the U.S. team. It was an eloquent rebuttal to the Nazi notion of a dominant "master race." Bob Beamon's incredible long jump in Mexico City was one giant leap for all mankind. The athletes who compete at the Olympic Games are explorers, testing the outer boundaries of human strength, speed and endurance against the limitations of distance, time, gravity and pain. To present these achievements only in terms of a competition for medals between nations belittles those efforts. And it belittles the efforts of those gifted athletes who, with courage and enormous investments in training, manage to place second, or fourth, or 23rd.

Everyone loves to cheer the underdog. So, when we convince ourselves that U.S. athletes are competing at a disadvantage, it makes their victories seem that much sweeter. By now, ABC has shown the taped replays of the Lake Placid "Miracle on Ice" a hundred times. The sight of our amateur hockey players exulting in their victory over the team of Russian professionals was a wonderful moment in sport—a victory against the odds. But we should remind ourselves that it tells us nothing about the superiority of our political system or the correctness of our foreign policy.

And we should remember that U.S. athletes are not as disadvantaged as U.S. sportscasters might portray them. Network reporters often describe our Olympians as handcuffed and hobbled by their dependence on private funding, while teams from other nations train with government subsidies. It is true we don't have direct government funding of our Olympians, but given the current state of government bureaucracy, that isn't necessarily a handicap. Even if it is, it's certainly offset by many other advantages.

Realistically, the U.S. team is not quite as disadvantaged as some sportscasters would have us believe. As one of the largest countries in the world, our team has a tremendous pool of potential competitors to draw from. Our athletes may not receive government paychecks, but they are products of a vast system of government-supported scholastic athletics with millions of participants, and they benefit indirectly from generous tax deductions offered to the private donors who support them.

NBC will undoubtedly show us how the East Germans and Soviets carefully screen their children for athletic talent and then train the best of them in a nationwide system of special programs. But doesn't our system of scholastic and collegiate athletics perform much the same function? After their scholastic careers, many of our most promising athletes are employed by major athletic apparel and equipment companies. And now, at last, U.S. athletes are eligible for direct payments from the U.S. Olympic Committee and can concentrate more fully on their training. We may have a lot to learn from Soviet physical education, but I still believe it's worth sacrificing a few medals so that our young athletes can retain the freedom to find their own success in the sport of their choice.

Most U.S. athletes have had the opportunity to grow up with adequate nutrition and sanitation, a prerequisite to build strong bodies and quick reflexes. At the age when our boys and girls are running on the JV track team, many of the world's children are already stooped over in a field, scratching out a meager subsistence for themselves and their families. Those many millions of potential athletes can't afford the luxury of training their bodies for sport. It is unlikely that the citizens of Mozambique, Honduras or Bangladesh think of us as underdogs.

In 1980 the United States and its allies boycotted the Moscow Games. In return, the Soviet Union and its allies boycotted the Los Angeles Games four years later. This year for the first time in twelve years, virtually the entire world will be represented at the Summer Games. Let's hope our broadcasters and print journalists don't diminish the event by turning it into another cold war skirmish.

I don't want to know how many medals the "Soviet Bloc" athletes have won and how that compares to the NATO medal count. I don't want to hear about the "medal gap" or a "window of vulnerability" in sports medicine. That kind of chauvinism is completely out of step with the spirit of the Games. It directly contradicts the feeling of international cooperation and mutual respect that so many athletes report experiencing during the Olympics.

The Olympic Games celebrate some of the best that is human: our ceaseless drive to greater achievement, and our ability to communicate and cooperate with one another despite our differences. A new Olympic record is a triumph for all humanity. Like the Apollo missions, the Olympics are one of those events that give us a broader perspective on our place and purpose. The Games remind us that we humans are one species, a species still struggling to learn how to share the gift of life on this planet. It will take both teamwork and tremendous individual effort for us to succeed in that struggle. Shouldn't that global perspective be the theme of this year's Olympic coverage?

Style Weekly, August 16, 1988

A Modest Proposal

Who doesn't love a three-day weekend? Even the U.S. Congress, not always noted for its collective wisdom, recognizes the value of three days off. Memorial Day, Martin Luther King, Jr.'s birthday, and "Presidents' Day" all now occur on Mondays by law, and the date be damned. And of course our legislators themselves make a habit of leaving town on Thursdays and not returning to their duties until Monday or even Tuesday of the following week.

A two-day weekend just isn't long enough. We spend Saturday catching up with chores put off during the week. We mow the lawn, vacuum, clean the garage, do the laundry, get the kids to soccer, shop, and attempt to finish all the other projects that have piled up during the preceding five days.

Sunday, for many, is a day for church and family. And in our high-speed world it's also the day to cook, do homework, and otherwise prepare for the onslaught of the next workweek.

Along with chores and responsibilities, we still try to squeeze in a little recreation too. We go out for pizza or a movie, listen to music, go to a game, or do a little reading. But before we know it, the weekend has evaporated and it's time to go back to work. There's just too much stuff to do each weekend to squeeze into two days.

This is a problem with an obvious solution. Let's

assume we're happy with our current level of productivity. We don't necessarily want to work less. We just need a little more weekend. We need an extra day. The answer couldn't be simpler. Add another day to the week. Presto! Three-day weekends.

We'd still have our five-day workweek. We'd have a day to get the chores done. We'd have a day for church and family. And in between, we'll have one extra day for rest, recreation and relaxation. Maybe we could even call it "Funday."

I know this idea will make some people uneasy. The Bible tells us the Lord created the world in six days, and on the seventh He rested. No mention of an eighth day in scripture. But few still insist on a literal interpretation of the story of Genesis. A day is the measure of the earth's rotation. What would even constitute a day before the earth was set spinning in the heavens? What is a "day" to the Deity anyway?

Of course, other religious traditions tell the creation story in entirely different ways. If the Biblical story of creation is symbolic rather than historically accurate, then we should be free to make rational adjustments to modern-day calendars.

Measuring time is a secular phenomenon, not a theological one. Science defines the second as 9,192,631,770 vibrations of a Cesium atom. Minutes, hours, days and weeks are all multiples of that standard. If we want to add an extra day to a week, we can.

Of course, moving to eight-day weeks would create a few other problems. What would happen to our months? The short answer is, "who cares?" Our current system of days and months is a mess—a hodgepodge of Norse, Roman and Christian elements. Seven of our present months have thirty-one days, four have thirty, and one has twenty-eight--usually. We can't even remember which is which without reciting a silly rhyme! A more rational alternative should be easy to devise. Here's one possibility:

Let's make months more uniform. Let's have eleven months, ten of which would consist of 32 days—four eight-day weeks. One month would have to include a fifth week. I suggest we extend May. Which month should we eliminate? That's a no-brainer. *Nobody* is going to miss February. Ten thirty-two day months and one forty day month gives us 360 days.

Or, if you prefer greater symmetry and a crisper break with tradition, we could divide the calendar into nine months, each consisting of five eight-day weeks. That too would total 360 days. Maybe we don't need months at all. We could just number the weeks from one to forty-five.

However, all these solutions have the same lingering problem. The earth revolves around the sun in *365* days. We need to account for five more days. Where should they go?

Add an extra day at the end of five different months to serve as our holidays: Martin Luther King Day, Presidents' Day, Memorial Day, Labor Day, and Veterans Day. Independence Day could just stay where it is, on July 4, no matter which day of the week it falls on.

Or we could stick those five days in the middle of

summer as an extra vacation for all of us! Call it "Summer Break." Or put them at the end of the year, between Christmas and New Year's Day as a universal winter holiday.

I know this sounds a little complicated, but it's not, really. It's just different. Certainly it's no more convoluted than the makeshift system we have now. Hey, after we get this little piece of business done, maybe we can finally finish switching over to the metric system.

(2004)

Solid Fuel

Finished, finally. Hurricane Isabelle took down dozens of large oaks around our house. Almost two years later, I finally finished cutting and splitting the last one. At least the last one within a few hundred feet of our side door. Isabel took down poplars and sweet gums as well as other oaks in the swampy woods behind our house. But those are simply going to stay there until they decay into the soil.

I haven't been in a hurry. The trees weren't going anywhere. I dismembered the one lying across the driveway immediately. Then I tackled two blocking the path our neighbors take when they walk to the park. The rest, I've worked on as time allowed—a couple of hours on a Saturday afternoon, or an occasional hour in the evening after I came home from work.

The last one was the biggest, and it was tricky. It was snagged in the crown of another tree, snagged at an angle of about $45°$. Too dangerous for my amateur lumberjack skills. Our local arborist put it safely on the ground so I could finish the cutting and splitting at my leisure.

So thanks to Isabel and a lot of hard labor, we now have a dozen piles of split logs neatly stacked near the house-- enough to last through the next couple of winters. The woodpiles are stacked carefully—straight and solid. I don't want a five-foot high load of wood teetering as I'm standing beside it, hoisting up the last piece.

We've heated with wood ever since we moved into our home 16 years ago. I quickly came to love the whole process of burning solid fuel. I love the smell of freshly cut wood. I enjoy the physical exertion of cutting and splitting, hauling and stacking the logs. The old New England adage that wood heats three times, once for the cutting, once for the hauling and once for the burning is an underestimate, excluding both splitting and stacking. It is serious exercise, easily the equal of a workout in the gym. After a couple of hours of work, I come into the house smelling of sweat and wood chips, chainsaw exhaust and oil--not an unpleasant combination, actually.

I love sitting in front of a wood stove on a chilly January evening. Our house has a heat pump, but it never quite makes us feel warm. But when the stove is stoked, you feel toasty, even on the coldest nights. In fact, we've learned not to start a fire when the outside temperature is above forty degrees. The heat will chase us out of the room.

I had to learn to cut wood. It's easy to make a mistake, and when you're toppling a 60-foot tree with a chainsaw, mistakes can be serious. Early on I misread the lean of a tree I was taking down. It clamped down on my saw blade as it started to fall in the direction opposite from the one I intended. I had to finish the job with an axe. Fortunately, it only cost me one section of a fence and a twisted chain bar when it finally came crashing down. Even when a tree is on the ground, it's easy to make a careless error. I force myself to wear steel-toed shoes, Kevlar chaps, leather gloves, ear protection and a face shield, even on hot days when shorts and a t-shirt would feel much more comfortable.

I love the satisfying, cracking "chunk" as the splitting maul—a cross between an axe and a sledgehammer--bursts a piece of oak in two. My Craftsman maul has an eight-pound, wedge-shaped head and a molded plastic handle. It has split a lot of wood over the years. Sears guarantees its tools for life, and this one is now in its third incarnation.

I've learned to use the maul like a karate chop— a full swing, with the kinetic energy of that eight-pound head focused *through* the wood. I've learned to look for the small cracks in the end of a log where the wood is ready to split naturally, and to aim for a centerline that passes through the heart of the wood. I've learned not to try to split through a knot—the maul bounces as if it struck concrete. And I've learned that when I start missing the centerline and losing the crisp snap of a focused blow, it's time to put away my tools and take a shower.

Different woods cut, split and burn differently. Red oak splits cleanly, releasing a sour smell strangely similar to aged cheese. An oak log will split apart with one well-aimed swing of the maul, almost as if you cut it with a knife. In the summer, the smell seems to draw yellowjackets as surely as a picnic does. White oak splits almost as easily. After a year of seasoning, oak logs produce long-burning coals. I can load our stove with dense, heavy oak before I go to bed, and still find enough embers to restart the fire the next morning.

In New England, rock maple is another preferred fuel.

The red maples that grow around here split easily, but their wood is lighter than oak, and burns hotter but not as long. We have plenty of sweet gums around the house too, and when a storm takes one down, I'll use it. Sweet gum wood grabs the maul blade and holds on to it, making splitting a chore. When it dries out, the wood is light and it burns too fast. But a big sweet gum tree is still too much fuel to pass up.

As for hickory, it's dense and burns long and hot, but it's misery to split. The fibrous logs fight every blow. We also have massive, fast growing tulip poplar trees on our property. The light colored wood cuts easily and splits beautifully. But you might as well burn rolled-up newspaper. Poplar melts away in a hot fire, leaving no coals, just fluffy ash. Cutting them for firewood is a waste of good sweat. And pine coats the flue with flammable tars that can eventually cause a chimney fire. Well seasoned, it does make good kindling, though.

I don't want to over-romanticize wood heat. It's a lot of work. And it's dirty. Every time we bring an armload of logs into the living room, we track in bits of crumbling bark and the occasional bug. Sweep or vacuum, and wood chips reappear on the rug five minutes later. Wood heat dries the interior air, even with pots of water steaming on the stove. And cleaning out the ashes, which I later spread on the garden, leaves a fine film of dust on nearby shelves and furniture.

How does our heating with wood affect the environment? Like most other environmental choices, it's a compromise chosen from a variety of imperfect options. Obviously wood smoke pollutes the air—a problem particularly noticeable on still, frigid days when the smoke forms a thin blue-gray haze above the house. If everyone heated with wood, the air would probably become unbreathable. But only a few homes in my semi-rural neighborhood do. And modern wood-burning stoves can be remarkably efficient, delivering two-thirds of the heat of combustion as useable warmth.

    Unlike gas or heating oil, wood is a renewable energy source. And the carbon from downed trees is soon going to reenter the atmosphere one way or another—if not from burning then from decomposition. So heating with wood is almost carbon neutral. Electric heat pollutes too, of course. We just don't see it. The exhaust from burning coal or natural gas pours out of stacks many miles away, far from the smoke-free appliances in our homes.

    So as long as my back and arms hold out, I plan to keep heating with wood. And on a chilly winter evening, you'll know just where to find me—comfortably curled up in front of the wood stove, enjoying the warmth I've paid for with my own hard work.

    (2005)

Is a Man's Best Dog

Pulling the Plug

About a five-minute walk from my house, one of our neighbors has erected his annual holiday display. The decorations started going up in early November, just as soon as his illuminated Halloween exhibit had been packed away. Our local Father Christmas doesn't limit himself to thousands of lights. His display also features hundreds of inflated, animated, illuminated plastic figures -- elves, polar bears, snow globes and snowmen. Of course, Santa, his sleigh and reindeer adorn the roof. There are also hundreds of unpowered ornaments, including giant snowflakes and white and silver "trees" — all illuminated with spotlights.

Don't get me wrong. I think simple, elegant holiday decorations are delightful. Small, green wreaths bedecked with red ribbon on the doors and the welcoming glow of electric candlelight in the front windows can magically transform a home. But decoration beyond that seems wasteful and, well, tacky.

I'm certain our neighbor's heart is in the right place. He's not trying to outdo the rest of us in some misguided frenzy of competitive electrification. He's not trying to keep us awake all night contemplating the birth of the baby Jesus with a bank of blinding, blinking lights. He is genuinely trying to bring us joy by celebrating the spirit of the season. On holiday evenings, he's often outside in a Santa suit, handing candy canes to children in the parade of automobiles slowly passing by, as they wonder at the splendiferous sight.

Of course, our neighbor is just one of many Richmonders participating in this yearly display of power consumption. Our local fish-wrapper of record recently put out a call for nominations to the 18th annual "Tacky Christmas Lights Tour." The minimum number of lights they require for entry: 40,000. Local television and radio stations eagerly promote this new "tradition" every December, as well.

Forty thousand light bulbs! It's time to pull the plug on this ill-conceived vulgarity. Haven't our media done a few stories about global warming over the past few years? Surely some intrepid reporter must have noted the mountains of coal piled at the Dominion Power station at Dutch Gap. Someone must have seen those tall smokestacks — the ones releasing tons of carbon dioxide gas into the atmosphere as the turbines generate power for all that superfluous illumination. Surely they've heard carbon dioxide is a greenhouse gas — it traps heat in he atmosphere instead of allowing it to radiate into space. It's an inevitable byproduct of burning fuel. As far as science can tell, while carbon dioxide in the atmosphere increases, so will our planet's temperatures. Obviously it would be wise to produce less of it.

Power-gulping holiday displays can't help. They're no small matter, either. I've done a ballpark estimate, using guidelines offered on the Environmental Protection Agency's Web site. Illuminating 40,000 small electric lights for the eight weeks of the holiday season will add approximately 100,000-200,000 extra pounds of carbon dioxide to the atmosphere. And that disregards the tons of extra fuel burned when thousands of us drive around town to gawk at the displays, as well as other environmental damage, including lung-damaging particulates ejected from those smokestacks, and mountaintops decapitated for the coal beneath the soil.

What could we do to put the brakes on this bad idea? Let's view those holiday displays with new eyes. We should explain the true costs and underlying ugliness of these sparkling displays to our children, who may delight in them even more than we do. In short, we should first choose not to participate.

Beyond that, we can try to educate the media, who seem incapable of educating themselves. Recently NBC — a subsidiary of General Electric, let's not forget — dedicated an entire week to environmental awareness. They turned their peacock logo green, and even broadcast a Sunday sports show from a studio illuminated by candlelight to show how much they care about energy conservation. Their local affiliate should take the message to heart. Stop promoting wasteful holiday illumination as feel-good stories during a slow news period. The other television and radio stations and newspapers in town should take similar stances.

Power companies could also discourage this kind of excess, I suppose. But that seems unlikely. They are in the business of selling electricity, after all. And late autumn is often a season of lower-than-average demand, when generating capacity is "underutilized."

What about the homeowners themselves? For some

neighborhood Santas, perhaps things have just gotten out of hand. They might welcome an opportunity to stop. You buy a few extra lights each year, and one or two more reindeer. Before you know it, friends want to know about plans for next year's extravaganza, and the ornaments start multiplying like bunnies. We should reassure them: We won't be disappointed if they cut back next year, and make a donation to Habitat for Humanity or the Salvation Army instead.

We would surely complain — or even call the police — if a neighbor were blasting loud music late at night, collecting junk cars and old refrigerators in the front yard, or otherwise making our local environment less hospitable. Are those nuisances so different from needlessly burning up natural resources, warming the atmosphere and melting the Earth's icecaps? Might we actually get the nerve to ask our neighbors to shut down their holiday lights?

Not easy to do. But if we're unwilling to speak directly, maybe we could slip a copy of *An Inconvenient Truth* into the neighbor's mailbox. That might convey the message. Or just send them a copy of this page. Consider it a holiday card from the planet.

Style Weekly, Nov. 21, 2007

In the Aftermath of Isabelle

It's been five years since Hurricane Isabelle roared through the Middle Atlantic states, leaving a new landscape in her wake. Behind our house, Isabelle uprooted hundreds of mature oaks and other trees. In some places, they fell like dominoes, the weight of each falling giant toppling the next.

But in the aftermath of destruction has come regeneration. The rebirth began immediately after the storm, and is continuing with each new day.

After the storm, the woods were cratered with shallow depressions where shallow roots once gripped the soil. Leaves wilted and died on the carcasses of fallen trees. Large sections of the forest canopy were ripped open, flooding the forest floor with sunlight.

The depressions left behind by the uprooted trees filled with rainwater, silt and humus. They became shallow vernal pools, green with algae after the spring rains. Insect larvae—including mosquito wigglers—and tadpoles swarmed in the warm, nutrient-rich water. The population of frogs and toads increased noticeably, and the nights grew full of croaking, peeping mating calls. Some of these pools, now filled with rotting leaves and other organic matter, have become mossy bogs.

Isabelle was a great boon for creatures that feast on dead and dying trees. Termites and fungi are gradually returning the nutrients in the massive trunks to the earth. In ten more years, the great oaks will be reduced to crumbly brown soil. In the meantime, the rotting wood houses millions of ants, beetles and pillbugs, as well as the occasional raccoon or chipmunk.

Where the canopy was torn away, the forest floor received direct sunlight for the first time in many years. The contrast between these clearings and the sections of forest where the canopy remained intact is dramatic. Only a few low plants manage to survive in the leaf litter under the shade of the great oaks. But in the new clearings, a profusion of young plants now reach upward, gathering as much light as they can.

The low-growing grasses and broadleaf weeds that first colonized the new clearings have already been overtaken by taller plants. These sunny spots are full of blackberry vines, sassafras saplings and pokeweed. Wild scuppernong and poison ivy vines are already climbing the young plants, seeking their share of the light. Thousands of saplings strain towards the light. Many of these young trees are now more than fifteen feet tall. Their race upward is a matter of survival. Only a tiny fraction of the plants growing in these thickets will survive long enough to flower and produce seeds. The others, shaded by their faster competitors, will die and return their own matter to the soil.

The profusion of new plants supports a new fauna as well. Squirrels and turkeys will have fewer acorns to gather for the next several decades. With an abundance of young plants to browse on, deer thrive at the woodland's edge.

Populations of insects that feed on the young plants in the clearings have exploded. Fuzzy white scale insects and aphids crowd the growing tips of many young plants. Caterpillars graze on the new foliage. And there seem to be more lightning bugs sparkling in the summer darkness than there have been for years.

Predators that feed on the burgeoning insect population are more numerous too. The clearings are busy with wasps, yellowjackets and web-weaving spiders. Insect-eating songbirds seem to be thriving. At twilight, squadrons of bats dart back and forth across the clearings hunting nocturnal insects.

The riotous new growth reminds me of just how amazingly resilient life is, even in the face of disaster. As the environment changes, some creatures disappear. But others arrive to take advantage of niches that the new conditions make available. I find this resilience reassuring, as I look at the discouraging signs of our own human presence on the planet.

Humans are remarkably adaptable. We've managed to establish ourselves almost everywhere on Earth, from tropic heat to arctic ice, from dripping rainforests to parched deserts. And as we've spread around the world, we've consumed more and more resources, prompting the extinction of thousands of other species great and small. Our species has roared across the face of the planet like a hurricane.

No creature deliberately sets out to eliminate the resources it needs to survive. It's the nature of every species to exploit its environment and reproduce more of its own kind. But nature put limits on such expansion. Algal blooms provide a simple example: If there's an abundance of plant nutrients—nitrates and phosphates--in a body of water, the algae population can explode. The single-celled phytoplankton thrive, dividing and re-dividing. But eventually, doomed by their own success, they deplete the food supply. The population crashes. Dead algae sink to the bottom, consuming the water's oxygen as billions of tiny organisms decay.

As the human population expands and pushes up against the limits of the planet's finite resources, it's easy to imagine our own species heading for such a crash. We're awfully ingenious, so advances in human technology may be able to stave it off for some time yet. And we do have the benefit of intellectual understanding. Perhaps we still have time to develop the wisdom to curtail our exploitation of the environment.

Even if we achieve zero population growth it seems unlikely that the Earth can sustain billions of human beings through the coming centuries. Our own population crash may come through famine, pandemic, war, climate change, some combination of those disasters, or by some new and as yet unforeseen catastrophe. Our species may not decrease to the point of extinction, but—barring some as yet unimagined, extraordinary leap in technology--it will probably contract to drastically smaller, sustainable numbers.

Given that prospect, I find comfort in watching what's

happening in the woodland clearings left by Isabelle. In the aftermath of great destruction, living creatures of all sorts and sizes have already begun repopulating and restoring the damaged environment.

Like all other species, *Homo sapiens* is a transient phenomenon. But our own exit from the planet is very likely to leave a living world behind. Life itself, in all its wonderful diversity, has survived and prospered on Earth for three and a half billion years. From the perspective of that time scale, human existence is just the faintest twinkle of a firefly.

(2008)

www.ingramcontent.com/pod-product-compliance
Lightning Source LLC
Chambersburg PA
CBHW070605300426
44113CB00010B/1407